RISING STARS
Mathematics

Year 3

Concept developed by
Caroline Clissold and Cherri Moseley

Year 3 Author Team
Caroline Clissold, Belle Cottingham,
Steph King

Pupil Textbook

The Publishers would like to thank the following for permission to reproduce copyright material.

Photo credits

Pages 10–11: sweets – Ivonne Wierink/Shutterstock; child – Brian A Jackson/Shutterstock; raffle tickets – chrisdorney/Shutterstock; money boxes – Aslan Alphan/iStock; page 23: Fibonacci – Public Domain; pages 24–5: cats – Linn Currie/Shutterstock; curry – Tiramisu Studio/Shutterstock; doll's house - Mike Flippo/Shutterstock; scooter – ffolas/Shuttersyock; table football – Jiri Vaclavek/Shutterstock; trampoline - rarach/Shutterstock; teddy bears - Preartiq/Shutterstock; pencils – Jochen Schoenfeld/Shutterstock; page 33: Mount Everest – Daniel Prudek/Shutterstock; pages 34–5: jars - zazamara/iStock; elephant – Donovan van Staden/Shutterstock; giraffes – DaddyBit/Shutterstock; milk cartons – ybmd/Shutterstock; hats – Polyryaz/Shutterstock; scarves – DJ Srki/Shutterstock; page 45: dictionary – adventtr/iStock; pages 46–7: child with snowball – Catalin Petolea/Shutterstock; sandcastle – Aneurysm/iStock; metallic spheres – Lucky/Photo/Shutterstock; girl in box – MarkHatfield/iStock; road sign (top) – George Clerk/iStock; road sign (bottom) - Liz Leyde/iStock; page 55: bird - Vladislav S/Shutterstock; pages 56–7: scales - DonNichols/iStock; gameboard – S McTeir; clock - Dimedrol68/Shutterstock; coins – claudiodivizia/iStock; pages 68–9: coins - claudiodivizia/iStock; skipping rope – Africa Studio/Shutterstock; signpost - mattjeacock/iStock; Houses of Parliament – S. Borisov/Shutterstock; clock – Evgeniy1/iStock; page 77: giraffes – Kamira/Shutterstock; pages 78–9: rowers - Ivan Smuk/Shutterstock (top); rowers – technotr/iStock (bottom); London bus - Aubrey Morandarte via Flickr (https://creativecommons.org/licenses/by-sa/2.0/); skittles – daseaford/Shutterstock; toy spiders – Niki Crucillo/Shutterstock ; toy cars – Kolopach/Shutterstock; apples – Evlakhiv Valeriy/Shutterstock; paper bags – infografick/Shutterstock; eggs – Oliver Hoffmann/Shutterstock; pets – Eric Isselee/Shutterstock; page 101: map - Google; pages 102–3: toy train – Murat Sen/iStock; child on climbing frame – Cheryl Casey/Shutterstock; London Eye - Courtesy of Khamtran via Wikipedia; girls skating – Johnny Greig/iStock; sunset – Giancarlo Liguori/Shutterstock; tall building – mtcurado/iStock; page 111: Agora Garden – Vincent Callebaut/Wikipedia Commons; pages 112–13: sack of rice – Evan Lorne/Shutterstock; departure board – byvalet/Shutterstock; key pad – Przemyslaw Ceynowa/Shutterstock; page 121: sundial – Elfstrom/iStock; pages 122–3: £1 and 20p coins - claudiodivizia/iStock; 10p coin – S McTeir; stationery – S McTeir; train carriage – Creative Images/Shutterstock; clock – ConstantinosZ/Shutterstock; basketball game – Gennadiy Titkov/Shutterstock; pages 132–3: house numbers – defotoberg/Shutterstock; coins - claudiodivizia/iStock; bottle of orange juice – SOMMAI/Shutterstock; windows - Jerges-Varga Ferenc/Shutterstock; page 143: ruler – Yotsatorn Laonalonglit/Shutterstock; pages 144–5: plants – photoiconix/Shutterstock (top left); plants – Simic Vojislav/Shutterstock(top centre); plants – Geo-grafika/Shutterstock (top right); plants – Sever180/Shutterstock (bottom left); plants – Vlue/Shutterstock (bottom right); juice carton – S McTeir; chess board – bluestocking/Shutterstock; courgettes – Peter Zijlstra/Shutterstock; 10p coins – S McTeir; all other coins - claudiodivizia/iStock; page 153: al-Khwarizmi – Wiki Commons; pages 154–5: formal garden – Jose Ignacio Soto; children with parachute – SolStock/iStock; children on bicycles – S McTeir; card – S McTeir; page 163: Burntwood - BrownhillsBoy - Wikipedia Commons (Creative Commons Attribution-Share Alike 4.0 International Licence).

Acknowledgements

The reasoning skills on page 8 are based on John Mason's work on mathematical powers. See Mason, J. and Johnston-Wilder, S. (Eds.) (2004). Learners powers. *Fundamental constructs in Mathematics Education*. London: Routledge Falmer. 115–142.

Every effort has been made to trace all copyright holders, but if any have been inadvertently overlooked, the Publishers will be pleased to make the necessary arrangements at the first opportunity.

Although every effort has been made to ensure that website addresses are correct at time of going to press, Rising Stars cannot be held responsible for the content of any website mentioned in this book. It is sometimes possible to find a relocated web page by typing in the address of the home page for a website in the URL window of your browser.

Hachette UK's policy is to use papers that are natural, renewable and recyclable products and made from wood grown in sustainable forests. The logging and manufacturing processes are expected to conform to the environmental regulations of the country of origin.

ISBN: 978 1 78339 524 8

Text, design and layout © Rising Stars UK Ltd 2016

First published in 2016 by

Rising Stars UK Ltd, part of Hodder Education,

An Hachette UK Company

Carmelite House

50 Victoria Embankment

London EC4Y 0DZ

www.risingstars-uk.com

Authors: Caroline Clissold, Belle Cottingham, Steph King

Programme consultants: Caroline Clissold, Cherri Moseley, Paul Broadbent

Publishers: Fiona Lazenby and Alexandra Riley

Editorial: Kate Baxter, Jane Carr, Sarah Chappelow, Jan Fisher, Lucy Hyde, Jackie Mace, Jane Morgan, Christine Vaughan

Project manager: Sue Walton

Series and character design: Steve Evans

Illustrations by Steve Evans

Cover design: Steve Evans and Words & Pictures

Printed by Liberduplex, Barcelona

A catalogue record for this title is available from the British Library.

Contents

Introduction

Hello, I'm Mia. Welcome to *Rising Stars Mathematics!*

Look at the pictures at the beginning of the unit. Think about the mathematics you can see in the world around you.

Talk about the questions with your friends. Do you agree the answers?

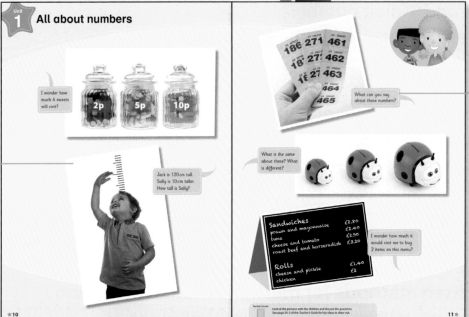

Read what Mia and Oli say. Can you spot if they have made a mistake?

Read the text and look at the diagrams to learn new maths skills. Your teacher will explain them.

Do these activities to practise what you have lear... Write the answers in yo exercise boo...

These questi... will help you explore and investigate maths. You w... need to think about them carefully.

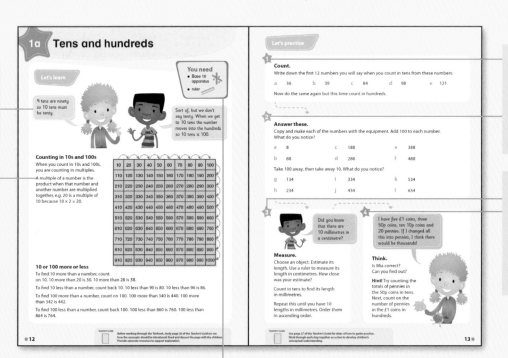

Use these items to help you. Make sure you have everything you need.

And I'm Oli. We'll help you as you learn with this book!

Play the game at the end of the unit to practise what you have learnt.

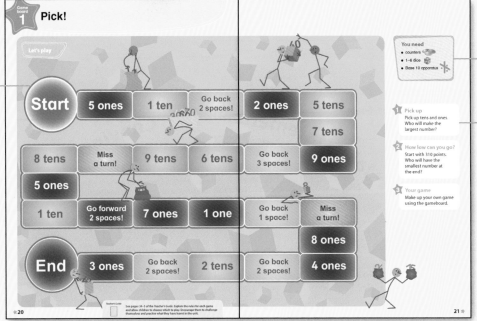

Make sure you have everything you need.

Follow the instructions to use the gameboard in different ways.

Try these activities to check what you have learnt in the unit. Have you understood all the new maths concepts?

Find out more about maths by reading these fun facts!

Problem solving and reasoning

Try these ideas to develop your reasoning skills. Doing this will help you improve your mathematical thinking.

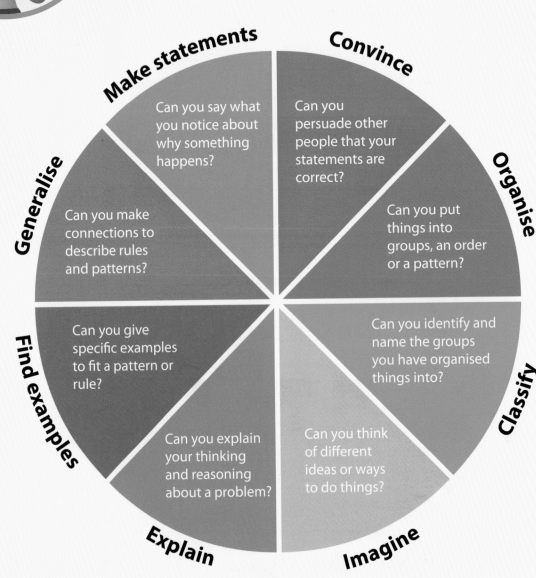

Make statements — Can you say what you notice about why something happens?

Convince — Can you persuade other people that your statements are correct?

Organise — Can you put things into groups, an order or a pattern?

Classify — Can you identify and name the groups you have organised things into?

Imagine — Can you think of different ideas or ways to do things?

Explain — Can you explain your thinking and reasoning about a problem?

Find examples — Can you give specific examples to fit a pattern or rule?

Generalise — Can you make connections to describe rules and patterns?

1 Read the problem carefully.

2 What do you need to find out?

3 What data or information is given in the problem?

4 What data or information do you need to use?

5 Make a plan for what to do.

6 Follow your plan to find the answer.

7 Check your answer. Is it correct? Put your answer into the problem to see if it works with the information given.

8 Evaluate your method. How could you improve it next time?

All about numbers

I wonder how much 4 sweets will cost?

Jack is 120 cm tall. Sally is 10 cm taller. How tall is Sally?

What can you say about these numbers?

What is the same about these? What is different?

Sandwiches
prawn and mayonnaise £2.80
tuna £2.40
cheese and tomato £2.90
roast beef and horseradish £3.20

Rolls
cheese and pickle £1.40
chicken £2

I wonder how much it would cost me to buy 2 items on this menu?

Teacher's Guide
Look at the pictures with the children and discuss the questions.
See page 24–5 of the *Teacher's Guide* for key ideas to draw out.

11 ★

Tens and hundreds

Let's learn

You need
- Base 10 apparatus
- ruler

9 tens are ninety so 10 tens must be tenty.

Sort of, but we don't say tenty. When we get to 10 tens the number moves into the hundreds so 10 tens is 100.

Counting in 10s and 100s

When you count in 10s and 100s, you are counting in multiples.

A multiple of a number is the product when that number and another number are multiplied together, e.g. 20 is a multiple of 10 because $10 \times 2 = 20$.

10	20	30	40	50	60	70	80	90	100
110	120	130	140	150	160	170	180	190	200
210	220	230	240	250	260	270	280	290	300
310	320	330	340	350	360	370	380	390	400
410	420	430	440	450	460	470	480	490	500
510	520	530	540	550	560	570	580	590	600
610	620	630	640	650	660	670	680	690	700
710	720	730	740	750	760	770	780	790	800
810	820	830	840	850	860	870	880	890	900
910	920	930	940	950	960	970	980	990	1000

10 or 100 more or less

To find 10 more than a number, count on 10. 10 more than 20 is 30. 10 more than 28 is 38.

To find 10 less than a number, count back 10. 10 less than 90 is 80. 10 less than 96 is 86.

To find 100 more than a number, count on 100. 100 more than 340 is 440. 100 more than 342 is 442.

To find 100 less than a number, count back 100. 100 less than 860 is 760. 100 less than 864 is 764.

Teacher's Guide

Before working through the *Textbook*, study page 26 of the *Teacher's Guide* to see how the concepts should be introduced. Read and discuss the page with the children. Provide concrete resources to support exploration.

1

Count.

Write down the first 12 numbers you will say when you count in tens from these numbers:

a   36   b   39   c   84   d   98   e   121

Now do the same again but this time count in hundreds.

2

Answer these.

Copy and make each of the numbers with the equipment. Add 100 to each number. What do you notice?

a   8   c   188   e   388

b   88   d   288   f   488

Take 100 away, then take away 10. What do you notice?

g   134   i   334   k   534

h   234   j   434   l   634

3

Did you know that there are 10 millimetres in a centimetre?

Measure.

Choose an object. Estimate its length. Use a ruler to measure its length in centimetres. How close was your estimate?

Count in tens to find its length in millimetres.

Repeat this until you have 10 lengths in millimetres. Order them in ascending order.

4

I have five £1 coins, three 50p coins, ten 10p coins and 20 pennies. If I changed all this into pennies, I think there would be thousands!

Think.

Is Mia correct?
Can you find out?

Hint! Try counting the totals of pennies in the 50p coins in tens. Next, count on the number of pennies in the £1 coins in hundreds.

Teacher's Guide

See page 27 of the *Teacher's Guide* for ideas of how to guide practice. Work through each step together as a class to develop children's conceptual understanding.

Hundreds, tens and ones

Let's learn

My guinea pig weighs seventy-five hundred and five grams.

That would be a very heavy guinea pig! I think you have mixed up your hundreds, tens and ones. Your guinea pig probably weighs seven hundred and fifty-five grams.

Place value

3-digit numbers are made up of hundreds, tens and ones.

You can make a 3-digit number using Base 10 apparatus.

This is the number 755.

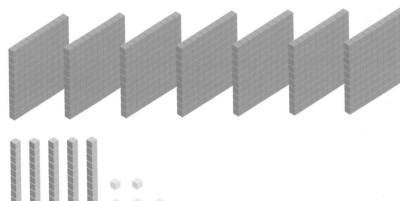

Place-value grids

A place-value grid tells you how many hundreds, tens and ones there are.

This grid shows the number 755.

Multiply each digit by its position to find its true value.

100	10	1
7	5	5

7 is in the hundreds position: $7 \times 100 = 700$

5 is in the tens position: $5 \times 10 = 50$

5 is in the ones position: $5 \times 1 = 5$

Now add all the numbers together:

$700 + 50 + 5 = 755$ or seven hundred and fifty-five

Teacher's Guide

Before working through the *Textbook*, study page 28 of the *Teacher's Guide* to see how the concepts should be introduced. Read and discuss the page with the children. Provide concrete resources to support exploration.

1

Write.

Make each of the numbers using Base 10 apparatus.

Then write the matching number statement, e.g.

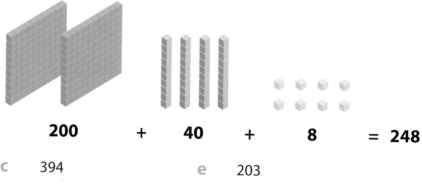

200 + **40** + **8** = **248**

a   189

b   213

c   394

d   486

e   203

f   600

2

Write.

Roll a dice 3 times.

The first number you roll is the hundreds.

The second is the tens. The third number is the ones.

Write a number statement to show what you did, e.g.

$300 + 50 + 4 = 354$.

Do this 6 times.

Which is the largest number you made? Which is the smallest?

Use a place-value grid to record your number!

3

Measure.

Use weighing scales to measure 200 g, 300 g and 400 g of sand into 3 plastic bags.

Do the same for 300 g and 400 g.

Choose 2 bags and predict the sum of their masses. Weigh them to check.

Write down their mass in numerals and words.

Do this twice more with different combinations of bags.

4

Think.

Roll a dice 3 times.

Use the 3 numbers to make a 3-digit number.

Use the same 3 numbers to make a different 3-digit number.

Decide which is larger.

Can you explain how you know?

Teacher's Guide

See page 29 of the *Teacher's Guide* for ideas of how to guide practice. Work through each step together as a class to develop children's conceptual understanding.

15

Comparing and ordering numbers

Let's learn

My bottle has a capacity of 395 ml and yours has a capacity of 410 ml. My bottle could hold more water than yours.

No, mine could hold more water. 4 hundreds is more than 3 hundreds. So I know my bottle has a greater capacity than yours.

Comparisons

Capacity is the amount of liquid a container can hold.

Volume is the amount of liquid that is inside a container.

You can measure both capacity and volume in litres and millilitres.

Look at the glasses.

They each have a capacity of 500 ml.

You can see that the volumes are different.

volume = 225 ml   volume = 475 ml   volume = 350 ml

Comparing and ordering numbers

Look at the numbers 225, 475 and 350.

The largest number in the hundreds column is 4. So 475 is the largest number.

The smallest number in hundreds column is 2. So 225 is the smallest number.

You can compare the numbers using symbols.

225 < 350 < 475   or   475 > 350 > 225

If the hundreds digits of 2 numbers are the same, look at the tens.

If the tens digits are also the same then look at the ones.

100	10	1
2	2	5
4	7	5
3	5	0

< means 'is less than'

> means 'is greater than'

Teacher's Guide
Before working through the *Textbook*, study page 30 of the *Teacher's Guide* to see how the concepts should be introduced. Read and discuss the page with the children. Provide concrete resources to support exploration.

★16

1

Compare.

Copy these number statements.
Use the symbols > and < to make them true.

a   234 ⬚ 243   c   222 ⬚ 333   e   433 ⬚ 343

b   243 ⬚ 203   d   244 ⬚ 242   f   343 ⬚ 334

2

Order.

a   Order these masses from greatest to smallest.

b   Use the symbols > and < to make up some comparison number statements.

267 g	150 g
360 g	400 g
460 g	205 g

3

Measure.

a   Pour different amounts of water into 3 different beakers.
Order the beakers from smallest volume to greatest volume.
Now use a measuring cylinder to measure the volumes.
Was your order correct?

b   Write number statements about these volumes using the symbols > and <.
Explain how you know that you are right.

c   Use your volumes to create volumes that are equal.

> You can add or subtract amounts to do this.

4

Think.

a   Use these numbers to make as many 3-digit numbers as you can. Work systematically.

b   Make 6 pairs of numbers and compare them using the symbols > and <.

c   Now take those 6 pairs and work out the 2 things that you can do to make the numbers equal.

Teacher's Guide

See page 31 of the *Teacher's Guide* for ideas of how to guide practice.
Work through each step together as a class to develop children's conceptual understanding.

17 ★

Representing numbers

You need
- ruler
- measuring cylinder
- coloured counters
- Base 10 apparatus
- number rods
- coins

Let's learn

10 is ten of something you can count, like 10 counters or 10 cubes.

Not always. We can show 10 in lots of different ways.

Representing numbers

There are lots of ways to represent numbers.

These pictures both show 125.

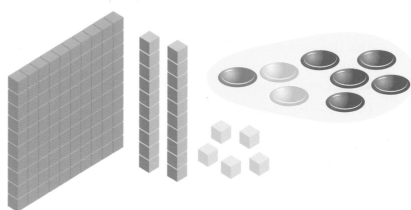

Numbers as measures

We also use numbers with measures.

These pictures show £1.25p and 1.25 kg.

1 kg

20 g   5 g

Teacher's Guide

Before working through the *Textbook*, study page 32 of the *Teacher's Guide* to see how the concepts should be introduced. Read and discuss the page with the children. Provide concrete resources to support exploration.

★**18**

1

Draw.

Make 150 in as many ways as you can.

Draw your different ways.

Compare your drawings with your partner's.

Which are the same? Which are different?

2

Show.

Take a selection of Base 10 apparatus including flats, rods and small cubes.

Estimate their total value and write it down. Next find out how much you actually have. Write this down.

What is the difference between your estimate and the actual value? Repeat 4 more times.

3

Measure.

a   How can you show 250 on a classroom ruler?
    Explain what you did.

b   How can you show 500 on a measuring cylinder?
    Explain what you did.

c   How many ways can you show 300 using money?
    Draw the coins that you used.

4

Think.

We see numbers all around us.

What numbers have you seen?

Think about the numbers you have seen outside of school over the last few days. Write down where you have seen these sorts of numbers:

a   money   d   mass

b   capacity   e   time

c   length

Share what you have seen with your partner. Are they the same? Are they different?

Teacher's Guide

See page 33 of the *Teacher's Guide* for ideas of how to guide practice. Work through each step together as a class to develop children's conceptual understanding.

19 ★

Pick!

Let's play

Start

5 ones

1 ten

Go back 2 spaces

8 tens

Miss a turn!

9 tens

6 te

5 ones

1 ten

Go forward 2 spaces!

7 ones

1 o

End

3 ones

Go back 2 spaces!

2 te

Teacher's Guide

See pages 34–5 of the *Teacher's Guide*. Explain the rules for each game and allow children to choose which to play. Encourage them to challenge themselves and practise what they have learnt in the unit.

2 ones | 5 tens

7 tens

Go back 3 spaces! | 9 ones

Go back 1 space! | Miss a turn!

8 ones

Go back 2 spaces! | 4 ones

1 Pick up

Pick up tens and ones. Who will make the largest number?

2 How low can you go?

Start with 310 points. Who will have the smallest number at the end?

3 Your game

Make up your own game using the gameboard.

Let's review

1

Oli wrote this number:

400203

That's four hundred and twenty-three!

Explain why Oli is wrong.

2

A mathematician named Caleb Gattegno made up grids like this one to help us to understand place value.

1	2	3	4	5	6	7	8	9
10	20	30	40	50	60	70	80	90
100	200	300	400	500	600	700	800	900

a   Use this chart to write 10 different 3-digit numbers below 500.
Write your numbers on a piece of paper.

b   Write your numbers in order, from smallest to largest.

c   Now write the numbers that are 10 more and 10 less than your numbers.

d   Write the numbers that are 100 more and 100 less than your numbers.

e   Choose any 4 of the numbers you have written and write them in words.

Teacher's Guide

See pages 36–7 of the *Teacher's Guide* for guidance on running each task. Observe children to identify those who have mastered concepts and those who require further consolidation.

3

a   Count in hundreds from 125 to 925.
Write down all the numbers that you count.

b   Think of 5 different ways to represent 125.
Draw them on a piece of plain paper.

> You could use counters, cubes, a number line, Base 10 apparatus or anything that you want.

Did you know?

The digits 1, 2, 3, … that we use today were introduced to Europe about 800 years ago by the famous mathematician Fibonacci.

Before that we used different symbols called Brahmi numerals.

1	2	3	4	5	6	7	8	9
—	=	≡	+	ҕ	Ψ	?	ﺱ	?

Mental and written calculation

Colour	Number of sweets
Red	
Pink	
Orange	
Yellow	
Green	
Blue	
Purple	
Brown	

Key: = 2 sweets

I wonder what this pictogram is about

I wonder how I can count these without counting 1 at a time?

Now £6.95
Opening deal!
£4 off
any
curry with rice

What was the original price?

Sale!

	Was	Now
Table football	£29.99	£14.99
Super scooter	£39.99	£19.99
Dolls' house	£59.99	£29.99
Trampoline	£24.99	£12.49
Family of teddies	£29.99	£14.99

How can I find out how much I will save on these toys?

If the shortest pencil is 5 cm long, I wonder how long the other pencils are?

Teacher's Guide
Look at the pictures with the children and discuss the questions.
See pages 38–9 of the *Teacher's Guide* for key ideas to draw out.

25 ★

Mental calculation strategies

You need:

- 100 square
- Base 10 apparatus
- interlocking cubes
- coins

To work out 46 + 28, I need to use a vertical partitioning written method.

You could use that, but a mental calculation strategy would be more efficient. You could add 46 and 30 then subtract 2.

Rounding to the nearest 10 and adjusting

You can add or subtract numbers that are close to a multiple of 10 like this:

To work out 46 + 28:

46 + 30 = 76   76 − 2 = 74

To work out 46 − 28:

46 − 30 = 16   16 + 2 = 18

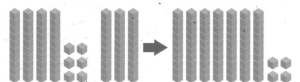

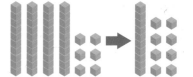

Bridging 10

You can also make 1 number into a multiple of 10. To do this, partition 1 number to make 2 numbers. One needs to be a number that adds or subtracts from the other to make it a multiple of 10. Look at these examples:

To work out 27 + 15, partition 15.

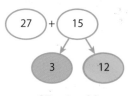

First add the 3:   27 + 3 = 30
Then add the 12:
    First the ones: 30 + 2 = 32
    Then the tens: 32 + 10 = 42
27 + 15 = 42

To work out 44 − 17, partition 17.

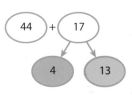

First subtract the 4:   44 − 4 = 40
Then subtract the 13:
    First the ones: 40 − 3 = 37
    Then the tens: 37 − 10 = 27
44 − 17 = 27

Teacher's Guide

Before working through the *Textbook*, study page 40 of the *Teacher's Guide* to see how the concepts should be introduced. Read and discuss the page with the children. Provide concrete resources to support exploration.

1

Calculate.

Add these numbers. Use the strategy of rounding and adjusting.

a   24 + 9   c   46 + 8   e   25 + 18

b   38 + 9   d   37 + 8   f   57 + 19

Subtract these numbers using the same strategy.

g   16 − 9   i   34 − 8   k   45 − 19

h   28 − 9   j   47 − 8   l   75 − 18

2

> Draw models to show what you are doing.

Calculate.

Add these numbers. Use the bridging 10 strategy.

a   46 + 7   b   65 + 28   c   78 + 16   d   86 + 34

Use the bridging 10 strategy or sequencing to subtract these numbers.

e   26 − 7   f   38 − 15   g   47 − 16   h   64 − 17

3

Apply.

Add or subtract these amounts of money.

Make the first amount of money using coins.

Choose whether you will use rounding and adjusting or bridging 10.

Add or subtract coins to check your answer.

Make the final amount using the fewest possible coins.

a   34p + 29p   c   56p − 9p

b   46p + 27p   d   67p − 28p

4

Think.

Oli had these coins.

He took 3 coins at a time and found the total.

Then he added 19p using the rounding and adjusting strategy.

He came up with lots of new amounts.

Write down the possible new amounts Oli could have found.

Teacher's Guide   See page 41 of the *Teacher's Guide* for ideas of how to guide practice. Work through each step together as a class to develop children's conceptual understanding.

27 ★

Developing written methods

Let's learn

I've worked out that 56 add 78 is 1214.

No it's not. If you think about it, 60 add 80 is 140 so the answer won't be in the thousands.

Addition

Look at this addition calculation.

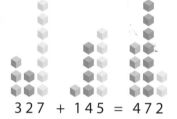

$$327 + 145 = 472$$

Vertical partitioning

Add the hundreds, then the tens, then the ones.

```
    3 2 7
+   1 4 5
    4 0 0
      6 0
+     1 2
    4 7 2
```

Short written method

Add the ones, then the tens, then the hundreds. $7 + 5 = 12$ so you exchange 1 ten into the tens column.

```
    3 2 7
+   1 4 5
    4 7 2
      1
```

Subtraction

You can use Base 10 apparatus to help you subtract.

You subtract the hundreds, then the tens, then the ones.

This example shows $243 - 128 = 115$.

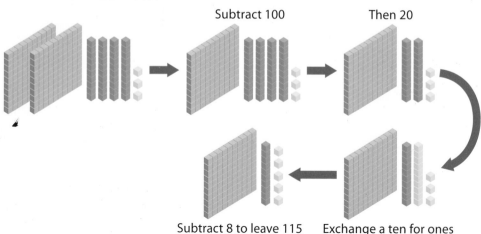

Subtract 100   Then 20

Subtract 8 to leave 115   Exchange a ten for ones

Teacher's Guide

Before working through the *Textbook*, study page 42 of the *Teacher's Guide* to see how the concepts should be introduced. Read and discuss the page with the children. Provide concrete resources to support exploration.

1

Calculate.

Answer these using Base 10 apparatus or cubes. Write the matching number statements.

a   145 + 136   b   168 + 126   c   157 + 169   d   243 + 174

Check each answer by taking the addend away from the sum.

Answer these using the vertical partitioning method.

e   138 + 125   f   167 + 142   g   187 + 214   h   268 + 134

Answer these using the short written method.

i   154 + 126   j   168 + 127   k   284 + 125   l   276 + 246

2

Answer these.

Use Base 10 apparatus or cubes to make each of these numbers.
Take 127 away from each number.
Write a number statement to show the minuend, subtrahend and difference.

a   154   c   186   e   275   g   325

b   174   d   243   f   281   h   302

3

Measure.

Use 2 metre sticks to make 6 different lengths that are between 1 m 50 cm and 2 m. Write these down on paper.

You need to subtract 1 m 12 cm from each of your lengths. Decide how you will do this.

Write a number statement to show each of your calculations.

Write a sentence to show how you found the difference for each.

4

I thought of two 3-digit numbers. The difference between them is 13. Both my numbers are between 250 and 300. One of my numbers is an odd multiple of 5.

What 2 numbers could Mia have thought of?

Write as many possibilities as you can find.

Teacher's Guide

See page 43 of the *Teacher's Guide* for ideas of how to guide practice. Work through each step together as a class to develop children's conceptual understanding.

29

Fish for sums and differences

Let's play

Start

Finish

Teacher's Guide

See pages 44–5 of the *Teacher's Guide*. Explain the rules for each game and allow children to choose which to play. Encourage them to challenge themselves and practise what they have learnt in the unit.

 Make it mental!

Find the sum of or difference between pairs of 2-digit numbers using a mental calculation strategy.

 Three digits

Find the sum of or difference between pairs of 3-digit numbers using a written calculation strategy.

 Your game

Make up your own game using the gameboard. Explain the rules and play with a partner.

And finally ...

1

Add these. Use the rounding and adjusting mental calculation strategy.

a $28 + 9$ c $65 + 18$

b $43 + 19$ d $78 + 28$

Check your answers using sequencing.

Subtract these. Use the same strategy.

e $58 - 9$ g $46 - 18$

f $47 - 8$ h $98 - 29$

For parts e–h and m–p, check your answers by adding the difference and subtrahend. Do you get the minuend?

Add these. Use the bridging 10 mental calculation strategy.

Draw models to show how you partition the addend.

i $24 + 7$ k $83 + 28$

j $38 + 14$ l $94 + 37$

Check your answers using sequencing.

Subtract these. Use the same strategy.

m $34 - 6$ o $47 - 28$

n $36 - 17$ p $81 - 45$

2

For each question, make the numbers using Base 10 apparatus or cubes.

• Use the equipment to show how to add the numbers.
• Write number statements to show your calculations.
• Then show how you have added the numbers using the vertical partitioning method.
• Then show the addition using the short written method.
• Finally, check your answer by subtracting the addend from the sum to see if you end up with the augend.

a $145 + 133$ c $168 + 128$ e $257 + 168$

b $263 + 131$ d $245 + 127$ f $367 + 284$

You need:

● Base 10 apparatus
● cubes

Teacher's Guide

See pages 46–7 of the *Teacher's Guide* for guidance on running each task. Observe children to identify those who have mastered concepts and those who require further consolidation.

3

For each question, make the first number using Base 10 apparatus or cubes.

- Use the equipment to show how to subtract the numbers.
- Write number statements to show your calculations.
- Finally, check your answer by adding the subtrahend to the difference to see if you end up with the minuend.

a   187 – 124

b   243 – 126

c   184 – 129

d   254 – 136

e   367 – 182

f   316 – 179

When you check your number statements, remember that subtraction is the inverse of addition!

Did you know?

summit

Many of the words we use in maths come from Latin.

For example, 'sum' comes from the Latin word *summa*, which means 'highest'. The word 'summit' comes from the same root.

33

Ways to multiply and divide

How can I find out how many jars there are?

I wonder how much taller this elephant is than me?

I wonder how much taller the mother giraffe is than the baby?

How can I find out how much milk is in each carton?

I wonder how many different ways I can put the hats and scarves together?

Teacher's Guide

Look at the pictures with the children and discuss the questions.
See pages 48–9 of the *Teacher's Guide* for key ideas to draw out.

35 ★

3a 2s, 4s and 8s

Let's learn

I don't see how doubling can help us learn our multiplication tables apart from our 2s.

Doubling helps a lot. We know our multiplication table for 2, so we can double that for our 4s and then double that for our 8s.

8		16		24		32		40		48	
4	8	12	16	20	24	28	32	36	40	44	48
2	4	6	8	10	12	14	16	18	20	22	24	26	28	30	32	34	36	38	40	42	44	46	48

Multiplication and division facts for 4

$2 \times 3 = 6$. You can double that to find $4 \times 3 = 12$.

Write out the multiplication table for 2. Double all your answers to make the multiplication table for 4. In the pictogram, each smiley face represents 4 children.

So there are $4 \times 7 = 28$ children in Class I.

You can use the multiplication table facts for 4 to find out how many children are in the other classes.

Class I	😊 😊 😊 😊 😊 😊 😊
Class II	😊 😊 😊 😊 😊 😊 😊 😊
Class III	😊 😊 😊 😊 😊 😊
Class IV	😊 😊 😊 😊 😊
Class V	😊 😊 😊 😊

Multiplication and division facts for 8

$4 \times 3 = 12$. Double this to find $8 \times 3 = 24$.

Double the facts for the multiplication table for 4 to make the multiplication table for 8.

You can use a triangle fact diagram to show multiplication and division facts.

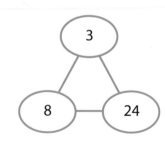

This shows:
$3 \times 8 = 24$
$8 \times 3 = 24$
$24 \div 8 = 3$
$24 \div 3 = 8$

Teacher's Guide

Before working through the *Textbook*, study page 50 of the *Teacher's Guide* to see how the concepts should be introduced. Read and discuss the page with the children. Provide concrete resources to support exploration.

Calculate.

Write down the multiplication table facts for 4 up to 12 × 4.

Then write down the multiplication table facts for
8 up to 12 × 8.

Explain to a partner how doubling can help you.

Now test each other on these facts!

Calculate.

Draw these triangle fact diagrams.
Fill in the missing numbers.

Then write the 4 number statements.
The first one is done for you.

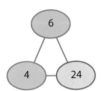

4 × 6 = 24
6 × 4 = 24
24 ÷ 6 = 4
24 ÷ 4 = 6

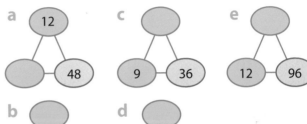

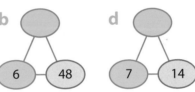

Measure.

Measure strips of paper to show the products of these multiplications.

a   4 × 3 cm

b   5 × 4 cm

c   8 × 2 cm

d   9 × 2 cm

e   4 × 8 cm

f   7 × 4 cm

Think.

Mia asked children in her class to name their favourite animals.

She drew this table to show her results.

a   Draw a pictogram to show this
     information. Choose your own symbol.
     Each symbol should represent 4 children.

b   Now make up 5 questions about it to ask
     a partner.

Animal	Votes
Elephant	20
Monkey	16
Lion	19
Snake	13
Giraffe	17

Teacher's Guide

See page 51 of the *Teacher's Guide* for ideas of how to guide practice.
Work through each step together as a class to develop children's
conceptual understanding.

37 ★

3b Commutativity

You need:
- Base 10 apparatus
- counters
- coins

Let's learn

I think that both multiplication and division are commutative.

Multiplication is, for example 6 × 4 is the same as 4 × 6. Division isn't though. 24 ÷ 4 = 6, but 4 ÷ 24 isn't 6.

Commutativity

Multiplication is commutative: same answer, different calculation.

Like with addition, you can multiply numbers in any order and you will always get the same answer.

If you know 6 × 4 = 24, you also know 4 × 6 = 24.

4 × 6 = 24

6 × 4 = 24

Arrays

You can set out a multiplication as an array.

The 2 arrays above show 4 × 6 = 24 and 6 × 4 = 24.

You can use the same arrays for division: 24 ÷ 6 = 4 and 24 ÷ 4 = 6.

Arrays can help you multiply larger numbers.

You could think of 23 × 3 = 69 as 23 + 23 + 23 = 69.

23 × 3 = 69

Use the array to work out 69 ÷ 23 = 3.

What other division can you work out using this array?

Teacher's Guide

Before working through the *Textbook*, study page 52 of the *Teacher's Guide* to see how the concepts should be introduced. Read and discuss the page with the children. Provide concrete resources to support exploration.

Calculate.

Use the numbers to make 2 multiplication and 2 division facts.

a   3, 4, 12

c   72, 9, 8

e   6, 48, 8

g   12, 96, 8

b   4, 8, 32

d   4, 36, 9

f   48, 4, 12

Calculate.

Describe each array as a repeated addition statement.
Now write a multiplication statement for each array. Work out the product using multiplication facts you know.
Next write the inverse repeated subtraction statements.
Then write a division statement for each array. Work out the quotient using division facts you know.

a

b

Measure.

a   Find a 5p coin.
How much would 4 times as many be? Put four 5p coins in a line to check. Can you make that amount using the fewest number of coins possible?
What about 8 times as many? Put eight 5p coins in a line to check. Now make that amount using the fewest coins possible.

b   Do the same for 6p, using the fewest coins possible.

Check by putting 5p and 1p coins in a row.

c   Make up your own amount and do the same again.

Think.

a   Write down 15 different multiplication and division facts that you can make from this statement:
$6 \times 3 = 18$.
Use doubling, halving and multiplying and dividing by 10.

b   Now do the same for 9×4.

Teacher's Guide

See page 53 of the *Teacher's Guide* for ideas of how to guide practice. Work through each step together as a class to develop children's conceptual understanding.

3c Sharing and possibilities

Let's learn

You need:
- strips of paper
- ruler
- scissors

We can't share 4 cakes between 8 of us.

Yes we can. We can halve each cake and we will each get half a cake.

Sharing

Sharing is a way of dividing that links to fractions.

The diagram shows 12 pound coins shared into 3 piles. There are 4 pound coins in each pile. Each pile is $\frac{1}{3}$ of the whole amount.

$12 \div 3 = 4$

$3 \div 12 = \frac{3}{12} = \frac{1}{4}$

Finding all possibilities

The diagram and table show all the possible different outfits you can make with 2 t-shirts and 3 pairs of shorts.

It is important to be systematic, so that you can keep track of what you are doing.

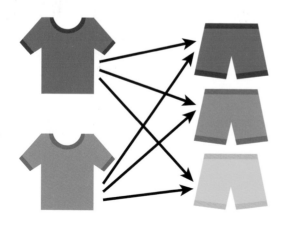

Teacher's Guide

Before working through the *Textbook*, study page 54 of the *Teacher's Guide* to see how the concepts should be introduced. Read and discuss the page with the children. Provide concrete resources to support exploration.

Calculate.

How much cake does each person get?

a   12 cakes shared between 3 people.

b   15 cakes shared between 5 people.

c   24 cakes shared between 8 people.

d   36 cakes shared between 12 people.

e   5 cakes shared between 10 people.

f   2 cakes shared between 8 people.

Calculate.

Work out the 2 quotients when you divide these pairs of numbers:

a   6 and 2   d   5 and 10

b   3 and 6   e   2 and 8

c   4 and 8   f   3 and 12

3

Solve.

Use coins to solve these problems:

a   Oli had £4.80. He shared it between himself and 2 friends. How much did each friend receive?

b   What if he had £5.46? £7.10?

Think.

I have 6 jumpers and 4 pairs of trousers. I can make 10 different outfits.

Is Oli correct?

Why did he think this?

Explain your thinking.

Teacher's Guide

See page 55 of the *Teacher's Guide* for ideas of how to guide practice. Work through each step together as a class to develop children's conceptual understanding.

Double trouble!

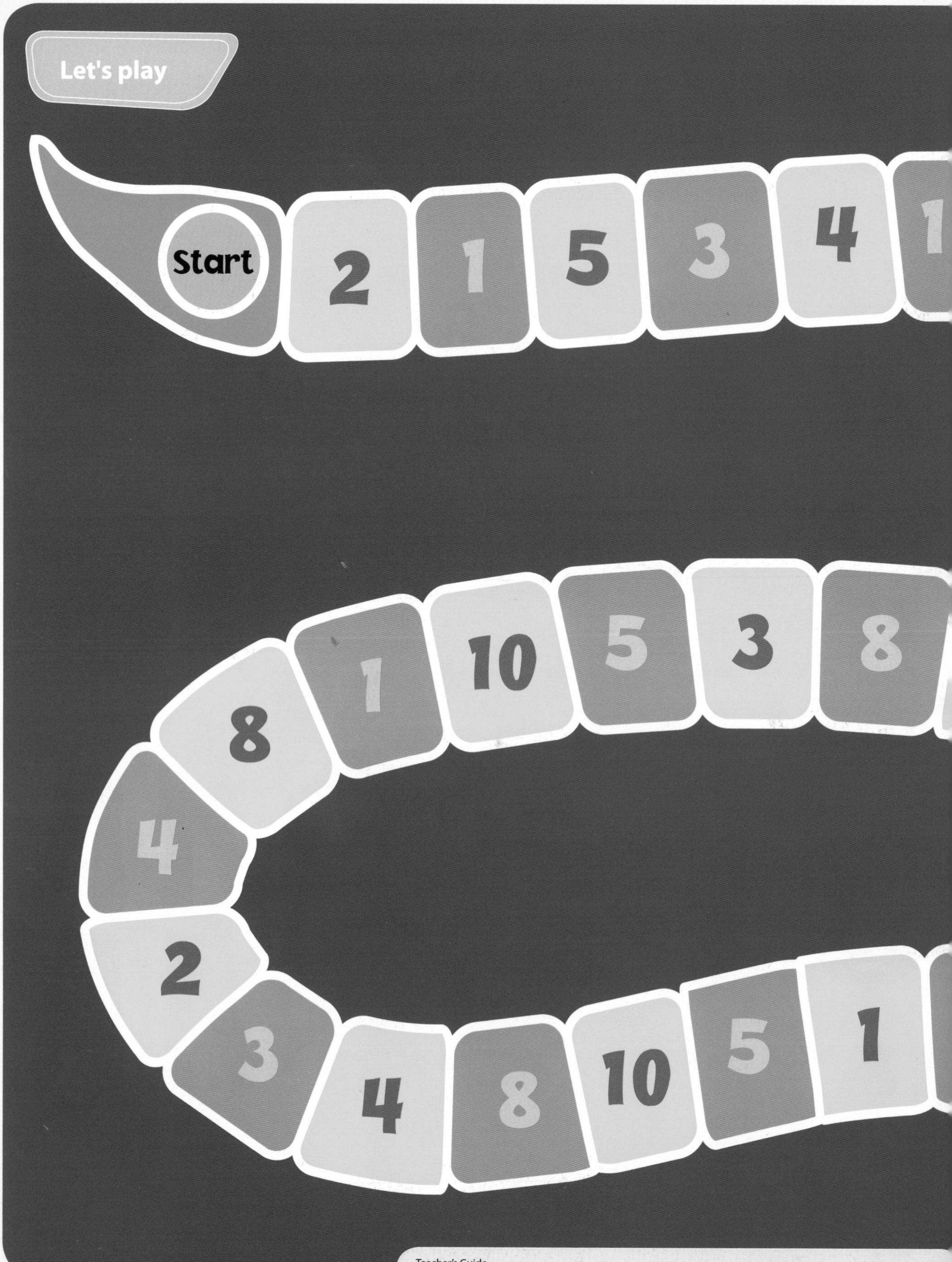

Let's play

Start 2 1 5 3 4 1

8 1 10 5 3 8

4

2

3 4 8 10 5 1

Teacher's Guide

See pages 56–7 of the *Teacher's Guide*. Explain the rules for each game and allow children to choose which to play. Encourage them to challenge themselves and practise what they have learnt in the unit.

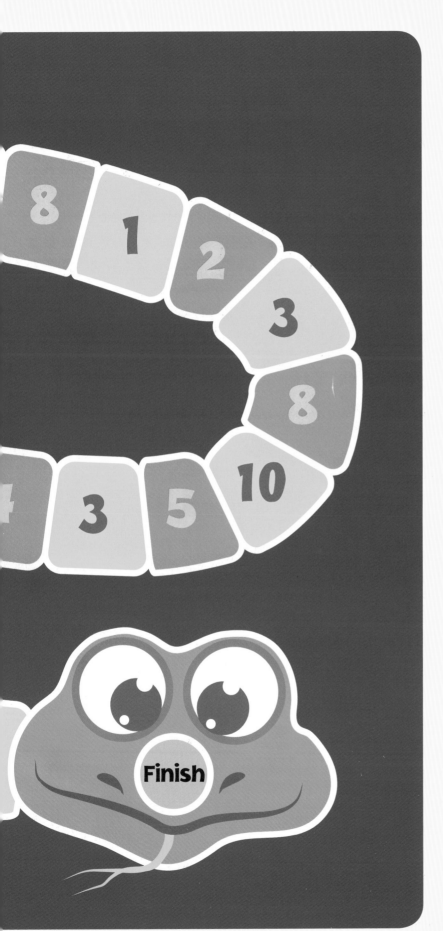

 1 Lots of facts

Generate as many new facts as you can in 1 minute.

 2 Doubling and doubling

Double and double again to score points.

 3 Your game

Make up your own game using the gameboard.

And finally ...

Let's review

1

Use Base 10 apparatus to make an array like this one.

You need:
- Base 10 apparatus

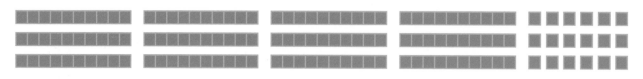

Add the tens and then the ones.

Now exchange 10 ones for 1 ten and 10 tens for 1 hundred.

What is your answer to 46×3?

Explain to a partner how you could also find the answer using known multiplication facts.

Now make up 4 other arrays using tens sticks and ones cubes.

Draw them and write the multiplication statements to describe them.

For each, describe how you could use known facts to check your answer is correct.

2

Take 32 counters. Make all the arrays you can.

Now write all the multiplication and division facts that you can for each one.

You need:
- counters

Choose 2 of your arrays and make up a problem, e.g.:

> Sophie baked 32 cakes.
> She put them equally into boxes.
> There were 4 cakes in each box.
> How many boxes did she have?

Teacher's Guide

See pages 58–9 of the *Teacher's Guide* for guidance on running each task. Observe children to identify those who have mastered concepts and those who require further consolidation.

3

Share 24 counters into groups of equal sizes.
Find all the possibilities.
Write a division statement for each one to show what you
have done. Write the fraction of the whole that each group is.

Do this again for 36.

Choose you own number to explore.

You need:

● counters

> How can you be
> sure you have found
> all the ways?

Did you know?

The French word
commuter means 'to
switch or substitute'.

The suffix -*ative* means 'tending
to'. So 'commutative' means
tending to switch or substitute.
That is just what you can do when
you multiply or add — switch the
numbers around and you will get
the same answer.

Angles and shapes

What shape is my snowball?

What shapes can you see?

What other materials can you use to make a cube?

How many right angles can you see?

Look at the angles in these signs. What is the same and what is different?

Teacher's Guide

Look at the pictures with the children and discuss the questions.
See pages 60–1 of the *Teacher's Guide* for key ideas to draw out.

47 ★

Making and describing 3-D shapes

You need
- 3-D shapes
- interlocking triangles, squares and cubes
- straws
- modelling clay
- squared paper

Let's learn

You need more interlocking cubes to make a cuboid than a cube because the cuboid is longer.

No, that's wrong! You need 8 interlocking cubes for both. They're just arranged differently.

Properties of 3-D shapes

A 3-D shape has vertices, edges and faces. A 3-D shape has flat faces or a curved surface or both. Vertices is the plural of vertex.

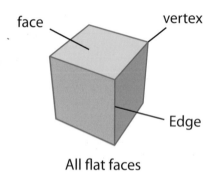

All flat faces

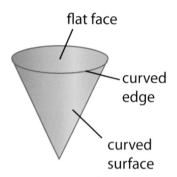

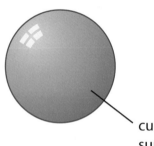

Making 3-D shapes

Different modelling materials can be used to make 3-D shapes.

This hexagonal prism is made from interlocking triangles and squares.

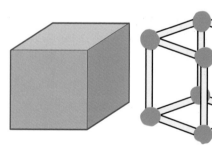

This skeleton cube is made with balls of modelling clay and straws.

Teacher's Guide

Before working through the *Textbook*, study page 62 of the *Teacher's Guide* to see how the concepts should be introduced. Read and discuss the page with the children. Provide concrete resources to support exploration.

Recognise.

Count the number of vertices and edges for each shape.

Copy and complete this table.

	Cuboid	Cone	Cylinder	Sphere	Triangle-based pyramid	Triangle-based prism
Faces						
Curved surfaces						
Curved edges						
Vertices						
Edges						

Group.

Look at these shapes. Copy and complete the bar chart.

How many more prisms than square-based pyramids are there?

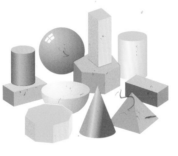

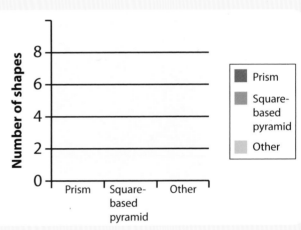

Make.

Make a skeletal model of a prism and a pyramid of your choice using straws and modelling clay.

Compare the properties of both shapes.

Think.

How many interlocking cubes do you need to add to the shape on the left to make it into a cube?

Make different sized cuboids using just 4 or fewer interlocking cubes. Draw and describe them.

Teacher's Guide

See page 63 of the *Teacher's Guide* for ideas of how to guide practice. Work through each step together as a class to develop children's conceptual understanding.

49 ⭐

You need
- 2-D and 3-D shapes
- coloured pencils
- a ruler
- straws

Let's learn

When 2 straight lines meet at a point, they make 1 angle.

Angle is a measure of turn. When 2 straight lines meet at a point, they actually make 2 angles.

Right angles

This is a right angle.
You mark a right angle like this.

The yellow angle is greater than a right angle.

The green angle is less than a right angle.

Identify angles

These shapes have no angles.

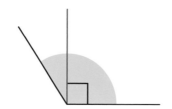

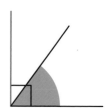

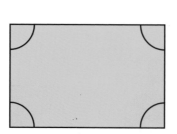

This quadrilateral has 4 angles.

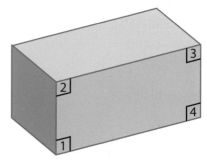

4 right angles are labelled on this box. Can you find any others?

Teacher's Guide

Before working through the *Textbook*, study page 64 of the *Teacher's Guide* to see how the concepts should be introduced. Read and discuss the page with the children. Provide concrete resources to support exploration.

1

Identify.

State whether each angle is a right angle, less than or greater than a right angle.

   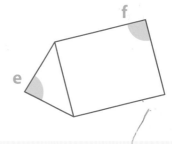

2

Answer these.

Look at the angles in the shapes. Copy and fill in the table.

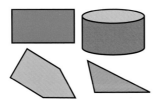

Shapes	Number of right angles	Number of angles less than right angle	Number of angles bigger than right angle
triangle			
quadrilateral			
pentagon			
cylinder			

3

Create.

a   Place 2 straws to make 1 right angle.

b   Place 2 straws to make 2 right angles.

c   Can you make 4 right angles?

d   Can you make 3 right angles? Explain your answer.

4

Think.

Draw 5 shapes, each with a different number of sides.

Mark and count the number of angles in each shape.

Copy and complete the table.

What do you notice about the number of angles and sides in each shape?

Name	Number of sides	Number of angles

Teacher's Guide

See page 65 of the *Teacher's Guide* for ideas of how to guide practice. Work through each step together as a class to develop children's conceptual understanding.

51 ★

Angles win points!

Let's play

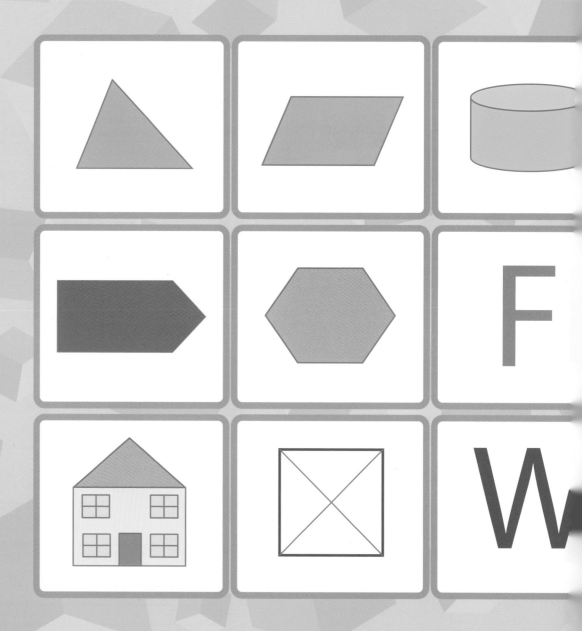

Teacher's Guide

See pages 66–7 of the *Teacher's Guide*. Explain the rules for each game and allow children to choose which to play. Encourage them to challenge themselves and practise what they have learnt in the unit.

1 **Three in a row**

Identify angles and place 3 counters in a row to collect points. Who collects the most?

2 **Three to make an L shape**

Identify angles and place 3 counters in an L shape to collect points. Who collects the most?

3 **Your game**

Make up your own game using the gameboard.

And finally ...

1

These shapes are grouped by the type of faces they have. Which shape does not belong in each group?

You need:
- 3-D shapes
- 2 hoops

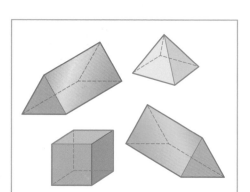

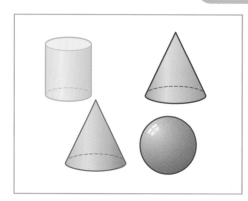

Mix the shapes. Can you think of a different way to group them?

2

Work in 2 groups to make as many angles as you can by drawing:

a   2 lines that cross each other

b   3 lines that cross each other

c   4 lines that cross each other

The group that makes the most angles wins the challenge.

You need:
- ruler
- different coloured pencils

Teacher's Guide

See pages 68–9 of the *Teacher's Guide* for guidance on running each task. Observe children to identify those who have mastered concepts and those who require further consolidation.

Use modelling clay to make:

a   a cylinder

b   a triangular prism

c   a sphere

d   a cube

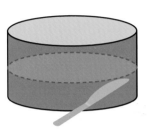

If I cut the cylinder in half, I will always have 2 smaller cylinders!

Is this always true?

Cut the other shapes in half. What shapes do you have?

Did you know?

Some scientists believe that baby birds begin to fly by learning to flutter their wings at a right angle.

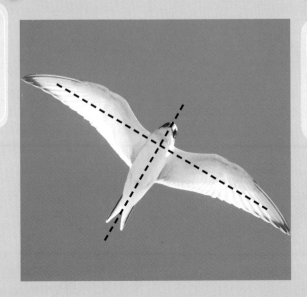

As they get older, they flap their wings at angles less than a right angle to speed up or when they're flying over steep objects.

Number and place value

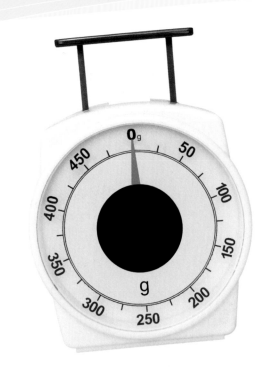

I wonder where 325 sits on these scales?

Can I roll the same number each time and still land on 30?

I need my rope to be 1 metre longer. How many centimetres should it be?

186 cm

I can count in steps of 5 minutes and in steps of 10 minutes. I wonder what times will be in both my counts?

I wonder how many pennies I have?

Teacher's Guide

Look at the pictures with the children and discuss the questions.
See pages 70–1 of the *Teacher's Guide* for key ideas to draw out.

57 ★

Counting in steps of different sizes

You need:
- 4 and 8 number rods
- 50p and £1 coins 50p £1
- Base 10 apparatus
- place-value counters 100 10 1

Let's learn

When I count in steps of 5 from zero, the ones digit in each number is 0 or 5 so the pattern will be the same for steps of 50.

No, that's not true. The pattern will only be the same for the tens digit. 50 is 5 tens and not 5 ones!

Counting in steps of 4 and 8

You can use number rods to help you count.

Look at the start of a 4 count and an 8 count.

8		16	
4	8	12	16

The numbers in both counts are all even because you are counting in steps of an even number from zero.

All the numbers in the 8 count are also in the 4 count because every step of 8 is made up of 2 steps of 4.

Counting in steps of 50 and 100

Continue this count of 50p coins.
What amounts do you say?
What patterns do you notice?

50   100

10 or 100 more or less

When you count in steps of 10 from zero the ones digit remains the same: 0, 10, 20, 30, …

When you count in steps of 100 from zero both the tens digit and the ones digit remain the same:

0, 100, 200, 300, …

The same rule is also true for counting in steps of 10 or 100 from any number:

104, 114, 124, 134, 144   23, 123, 223, 323, 423

You can use these patterns to help you find 10 or 100 more or less than any number.

Teacher's Guide

Before working through the *Textbook*, study page 72 of the *Teacher's Guide* to see how the concepts should be introduced. Read and discuss the page with the children. Provide concrete resources to support exploration.

Count.

Use number rods to continue these counts.

a   16, 20, 24, ___ , ___ , ___

b   0, 8, 16, ___ , ___ , ___

c   8, 12, 16, ___ , ___ , ___

d   40, 32, 24, ___ , ___ , ___

e   Which of these numbers will be in your count of 4 **and** your count of 8?

12   30   24   40   44   80   84   36

Calculate.

Use Base 10 apparatus or place-value counters to make these numbers:

156   208   393   950

a   Find 10 more and 10 less of each number.

b   Find 100 more and 100 less of each number.

Apply.

300	150	700
600	350	250
550	400	650

Pick different numbers from the grid. Use 50p or £1 coins to help record the count from zero each time.

For example:

300 → 0, 50, 100, 150, 200, 250, 300

300 → 0, 100, 200, 300

Think.

Oli has drawn this pictogram, but he cannot remember the scale he has used.

Mmm, I remember that Sami had 12 more stickers than Benna.

Benna	😊😊😊😊😊😊
Sami	😊😊😊😊😊😊😊◖
Asha	😊😊😊◖
Mia	😊😊😊😊😊

Find the scale that Oli has used for his pictogram.

Find the number of stickers collected by each child.

Teacher's Guide

See page 73 of the *Teacher's Guide* for ideas of how to guide practice. Work through each step together as a class to develop children's conceptual understanding.

59

5b Writing and comparing numbers

Let's learn

Three hundred and four is written in numbers as 3004. Look, you can see the 300 and the 4.

No, that's three thousand and four! You forgot that the 4 is a ones digit and replaces the second zero in 300.

Writing and representing numbers

The number 123 is written in words as one hundred and twenty-three.

123 can be represented in different ways.

hundreds	tens	ones
1	2	3

1000	2000	3000	4000	5000	6000	7000	8000	9000
100	200	300	400	500	600	700	800	900
10	20	30	40	50	60	70	80	90
1	2	3	4	5	6	7	8	9

You can use these representations to find 10 less than 123.
You write this new number as 113 and one hundred and thirteen.

Comparing and ordering numbers

These numbers are made up of the same 3 digits but their values are different.

567   657   576

You can use representations to help you compare and order the numbers.
Which 2 numbers are represented here?

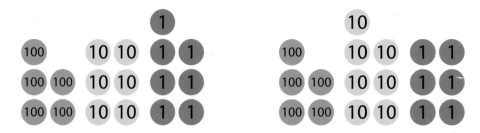

You can show how numbers compare using the greater than and less than symbols.
576 > 567 but 657 > 576.
The numbers can be written in order from smallest to largest as 567, 576, 657.

Teacher's Guide

Before working through the *Textbook*, study page 74 of the *Teacher's Guide* to see how the concepts should be introduced. Read and discuss the page with the children. Provide concrete resources to support exploration.

1

Read, make and write.

Take turns to read these numbers to your partner. Your partner must make the number using place-value counters or Base 10 apparatus. Then you write the number using digits.

a   Seven hundred and thirty-three

b   Four hundred and seventeen

c   Two hundred and ninety

d   Six hundred and five

e   Eighty-seven

f   One hundred and eleven

2

Make and order.

Here are 2 different numbers represented by place-value counters.

100 100 10   1
100 100 10 10 1 1

                    1
100   1 1
100 100 10 10   1 1

a   Use place-value counters to make at least 5 different numbers. Each number you make must use 10 counters.

b   What is the largest and smallest number you can make?

c   Pick 3 of your numbers and write them in order from smallest to largest.

3

Apply.

Find and compare the mass of different pairs of objects in the classroom.

Write the mass in grams (g) each time and use the symbols < or > to record your findings.

Write all your masses in order from lightest to heaviest.

4

Think.

Here is the start of a maths story for the number 123.

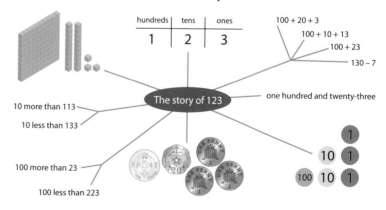

Choose 2 different 3-digit numbers and write a maths story for each number.

Teacher's Guide

See page 75 of the *Teacher's Guide* for ideas of how to guide practice.
Work through each step together as a class to develop children's conceptual understanding.

61

5c Tenths

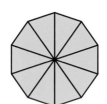

$\frac{1}{10}$ comes after $\frac{1}{2}$ on a number line because 10 is greater than 2.

No, $\frac{1}{10}$ is smaller than $\frac{1}{2}$. The whole is cut up into 10 equal pieces. Each piece is smaller than the same whole cut up into only 2 equal pieces!

one whole

Dividing by 10 to make tenths

When you divide an object, a quantity or a single-digit number equally, you make equal parts or fractions.

When you divide by 10, each equal part is called a tenth or $\frac{1}{10}$.

The number you divide by becomes the denominator in the fraction.

On a place-value grid, the position to the right of the 'ones' column is called 'tenths'.

10	1	.	10th ($\frac{1}{10}$)
		(1 ÷ 10)	
		.	1

You can make $\frac{1}{10}$ by dividing 1 by 10 $1 \div 10 = \frac{1}{10}$

You can make $\frac{2}{10}$ by dividing 2 by 10 $2 \div 10 = \frac{2}{10}$

Any fraction can be written as a division statement, so every division statement can be written as a fraction!

Counting in tenths

Just like halves and quarters, you can also find tenths on a number line.

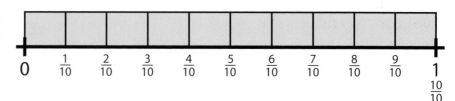

$0 \quad \frac{1}{10} \quad \frac{2}{10} \quad \frac{3}{10} \quad \frac{4}{10} \quad \frac{5}{10} \quad \frac{6}{10} \quad \frac{7}{10} \quad \frac{8}{10} \quad \frac{9}{10} \quad 1 \; \frac{10}{10}$

You can count in steps of $\frac{1}{10}$ up to 1 whole or $\frac{10}{10}$. What do you notice about $\frac{5}{10}$?

You can also continue to count beyond 1: $1\frac{1}{10}, 1\frac{2}{10}, 1\frac{3}{10}, 1\frac{4}{10} \cdots$

Teacher's Guide

Before working through the *Textbook*, study page 76 of the *Teacher's Guide* to see how the concepts should be introduced. Read and discuss the page with the children. Provide concrete resources to support exploration.

Calculate.

Use a place-value grid and digit cards to divide each of these numbers by 10.
Write the calculation you use each time.

a   4

c   7

e   Write the division statement that matches the fraction $\frac{8}{10}$.

b   6

d   3

Answer.

Which of these representations show tenths? Explain how you know.

a

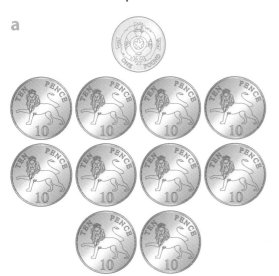

b

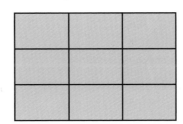

c

d

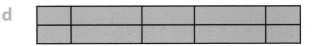

Apply.

Take a small handful of 10p coins.
Each coin represents $\frac{1}{10}$ of a pound.

Count the coins in tenths. When you have 10 tenths $\left(\frac{10}{10}\right)$, change them for a pound.

Record the last number in your count.

Repeat with different handfuls of 10p coins.

Think.

Oli counts on in tenths from $\frac{1}{2}$ each time.
Mia counts back in tenths from 2 each time.

Find out how many different ways Oli and Mia can make steps of $\frac{1}{10}$ so they both land on the same number.

I count on $\frac{5}{10}$ from $\frac{1}{2}$, Mia must count back $\frac{10}{10}$ from 2 so we both land on 1.

Teacher's Guide
See page 77 of the *Teacher's Guide* for ideas of how to guide practice.
Work through each step together as a class to develop children's conceptual understanding.

63

Digit decisions!

Let's play

	Hundreds	Tens	Ones
Player 1			
Player 2			

Teacher's Guide
See pages 78–9 of the *Teacher's Guide*. Explain the rules for each game and allow children to choose which to play. Encourage them to challenge themselves and practise what they have learnt in the unit.

1 Make it large!

Choose the position of the digit cards wisely to get a higher 3-digit number than your partner.

2 Small numbers

Make the lowest 3-digit number to win this game. Think carefully about where you will position each digit card.

3 Your game

Make up your own game using the gameboard.

And finally ...

1

> I am counting in steps of 50 from zero.
> Oli is counting in steps of 100 from zero.

a   Write **5** different numbers that both children will say in their count.
Write **5** different numbers that only Mia will say in her count.

> I am counting in steps of 8 from zero.
> Mia is counting in steps of 4 from zero.

b   Write **5** different numbers that both children will say in their count.
Write **5** different numbers that only Oli will say in his count.

2

a   Use digit cards to make a number that sits in the shaded part of this number line.
Write the number that is 10 and 100 more than your number.

Now write the number that is 10 and 100 less than your number.

You need:
- digit cards (0–7)

b   Rearrange the same 3 digit cards to make 2 other numbers.
Where will they go on the number line?

0–100	100–200	200–300	300–400	400–500	500–600	600–700	700–800

c   Now write the 3 numbers you made with your digit cards in order from smallest to largest.

Teacher's Guide   See pages 80–1 of the *Teacher's Guide* for guidance on running each task.
Observe children to identify those who have mastered concepts and those who require further consolidation.

Roll both dice to generate 2 numbers.

Choose 1 of the numbers for your step size in tenths and the other for the number of steps, e.g. you roll 3 and 4 and choose 3 for a step size of $\frac{3}{10}$ and make 4 steps from zero.

Write the numbers your counter lands on each time, e.g. $\frac{3}{10}, \frac{6}{10}, \frac{9}{10}, 1\frac{2}{10}$.

$\frac{1}{10}$	$\frac{2}{10}$	$\frac{3}{10}$	$\frac{4}{10}$	$\frac{5}{10}$	$\frac{6}{10}$	$\frac{7}{10}$	$\frac{8}{10}$	$\frac{9}{10}$	1

Did you know?

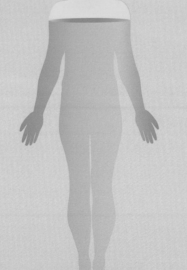

The fraction of water in a human body depends on a person's age, gender, weight and health. It is impossible to give an exact fraction that applies to all people.

In an adult, water makes up somewhere between $\frac{6}{10}$ and $\frac{7}{10}$ of the human body. A newborn baby is made up of just over $\frac{7}{10}$ water. Children and women usually have a larger fraction of water in their bodies than men.

Addition and subtraction

I wonder if there is enough money to buy the skipping rope?

£1.99

London - I am here

Sea Life Brighton 70 km

Cardiff Castle 243 km

Disneyland - Paris 340 km

If I choose one of these places to visit from London, how much further I would have to travel to reach 500 km?

Well done for arriving on time!

I wonder whether the school has started?

Number of dogs and cats at one time at Battersea Dogs and Cats Home.

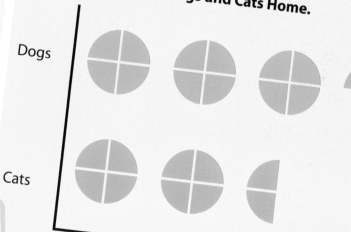

Dogs

Cats

Key:  = 100

How many dogs and cats are helped at Battersea?

Teacher's Guide
Look at the pictures with the children and discuss the questions.
See pages 82–3 of the *Teacher's Guide* for key ideas to draw out.

69 ★

Adding 3-digit numbers

You need
- place-value counters
- Base 10 apparatus
- calculators
- cards or sticky notes
- coins
- interlocking cubes

Let's learn

I have 30p less pocket money than you. I have 80p. Have you got 50p?

No, I have more money than you. I must have 80p + 30p = 110p or £1 and 10p.

Mental methods of addition

You can calculate 319 + 80 mentally in different ways:

Sequencing and adding

Count in tens from 319: 329, 339, 349, 359, 369, 379, 389, 399.

Partitioning and adding

First partition 319 to 309 +10,
80 + 10 = 90, 309 + 90 = 399.

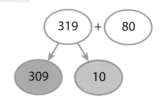

Adjusting and adding

Add the nearest multiple of 10 and then subtract the extra ones you have added.

319 + 80 = 320 + 80= 400, 400 − 1 = 399.

Formal written method of addition

328 + 516

300 + 20 + 8

500 + 10 + 6

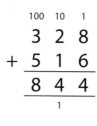

$$\begin{array}{r} {\scriptstyle 100\ \ 10\ \ 1} \\ 3\ 2\ 8 \\ +\ 5\ 1\ 6 \\ \hline 8\ 4\ 4 \\ {\scriptstyle 1} \end{array}$$

+

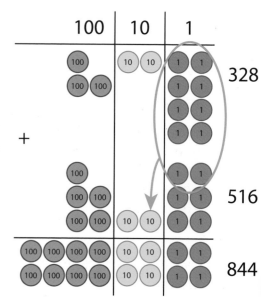

100	10	1	
			328
			516
			844

Teacher's Guide

Before working through the *Textbook*, study page 84 of the *Teacher's Guide* to see how the concepts should be introduced. Read and discuss the page with the children. Provide concrete resources to support exploration.

Add mentally.

Explain to your partner how your mental method works.

a   360 + 41   c   432 + 50   e   470 + 20

b   245 + 200   d   318 + 300   f   237 + 700

Copy and complete.

Use a written method to answer these.

a   417 + 222   d   523 + 28

b   417 + 25   e   531 + 203

c   234 + 151   f   434 + 27

Make an estimate to check your answers.

Apply.

Work with a friend. You are opening a shop.

Use 5 cards or sticky notes. Draw or write 1 of these words on each card:

ice-cream	apple
juice	
banana	sandwich

Place a price tag on each item. At least 2 of the prices should be more than £1.

a   Your partner buys 2 items from the shop. How much do they cost?
And another item?
And another?

b   You have £5 to spend. Calculate which items you can buy.

Investigate.

654 + 40 is more than 600 but less than 700.

Copy and complete.

a   309 + 60 is more than ▢ but less than ▢

b   138 + ▢ is more than 300 but less than ▢

c   ▢ + ▢ is more than 450 but less than ▢

d   ▢ + ▢ is more than ▢ but less than ▢

Check your answers by adding the numbers.

Teacher's Guide
See page 85 of the *Teacher's Guide* for ideas of how to guide practice. Work through each step together as a class to develop children's conceptual understanding.

Subtracting 3-digit numbers

Let's learn

You only subtract if the question says 'take away' or 'subtract'.

No! The question could say 'find the difference'. It could also ask you to compare how much more or less there is.

Mental methods of subtraction

Always see if you can use a mental method first.

Number line and subtraction

To solve 131 – 120 use a bar model.

131	
120	?

Then use the counting-on strategy on the number line to find the difference.

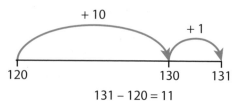

$$131 - 120 = 11$$

Formal written method of subtraction

To solve 682 – 56 a written method is needed.

In the ones column, it is not possible to calculate 2 – 6.

One of the tens has to move into the ones position to become ten ones.

Use addition 626 + 56 = 682 to check the answer.

Adjusting and subtracting

To solve 540 – 299 add 1 to 299 to make it 300
540 – 300 = 240. Add 1 back, 240 + 1 = 241.

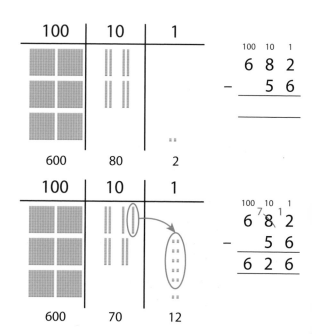

Teacher's Guide

Before working through the *Textbook*, study page 86 of the *Teacher's Guide* to see how the concepts should be introduced. Read and discuss the page with the children. Provide concrete resources to support exploration.

1

Answer these.

Make an estimate first.

Use a mental subtraction method.

a   471 – 200

b   576 – 300

c   105 – 98

d   830 – 110

e   200 – 170

f   776 – 759

g   Write the addition calculations to check your answers.

2

Copy and complete.

Use a written method to answer these.

a   374 – 108

b   480 – 59

c   673 – 38

d   374 – 47

e   £171 – £49

f   482 kg – 35 kg

g   173 cm – 39 cm

h   234 ml – 28 ml

3

Measure.

Work in a small group in the playground.

Measure how far each one of you can jump forward. Measure to the nearest centimetre (cm).

The longest long jump in the world is just under 9 m or 900 cm!

How far was your jump from the world record?

Compare 2 jump lengths.

Calculate the difference using a mental or written method.

How many different subtraction number statements can you make?

4

Investigate.

Use the numbers 1, 3, 4, 7, 8 once only to make one 3-digit number and one 2-digit number.

Subtract one number from the other to get:

a   the smallest answer

b   the biggest answer.

Show your workings clearly. Use addition to check your answers.

Teacher's Guide

See page 87 of the *Teacher's Guide* for ideas of how to guide practice. Work through each step together as a class to develop children's conceptual understanding.

Golden treasure!

Let's play

Start
419? 318?

20 or 200

Bury 13

30 or 130

Roll again

1 o

Go back 3 squares

Miss a turn
Sea Storm

Odd number under 80

Bury 50 or 150

Miss a turn
Sea Storm

Bur

Miss a turn
Sea Storm

Bury 16 or 160

Roll again

Bury a number under 100

7 or 17

5, 50 or 105

Bu
28 o

Teacher's Guide

See pages 88–9 of the *Teacher's Guide*. Explain the rules for each game and allow children to choose which to play. Encourage them to challenge themselves and practise what they have learnt in the unit.

Miss a turn
Sea Storm

Bury 100

Roll again

100

...ber r

Bury 30 or 130

Roll again

Bury 100

a

Bury 22 or 200

The End!
How many coins do you have?

1 **999 coins**

Race around the track collecting gold coins. Collect 999 gold coins first or have the most coins by the end of the game!

2 **Bury the treasure!**

Hide your gold coins by burying them away.

3 **Your game**

Design your own game using the gameboard. Explain the rules and play with a partner.

And finally ...

1

Solve these questions. Show your workings clearly.

Class 3A and 3B went on a school trip to the beach. They collected shells.
The data is shown in the diagram.

a   How many shells did they collect in total?

b   How many more shells did Class 3A collect than Class 3B?

c   The coach took 2 hours to get from school to the beach. The journey back was 10 minutes shorter. How long was the total journey to the beach?

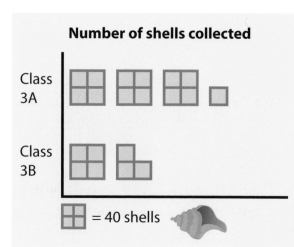

Number of shells collected

Class 3A

Class 3B

= 40 shells

2

Copy and complete the missing ingredients for 20 biscuits.

Making 10 gingerbread biscuits

You need:
1 egg
125 grams of butter
106 grams of sugar
110 grams of flour
5 grams of baking powder
2 grams of ginger

Making 20 gingerbread biscuits

You need:
2 eggs
? grams of butter
? grams of sugar
? grams of flour
10 grams of baking powder
4 grams of ginger

You have: 120 grams of butter, 320 grams of sugar, 337 grams of flour.

a   How much more butter do you need to make 20 gingerbread biscuits?

b   How much sugar and flour do you have left over if you make 20 gingerbread biscuits?

Teacher's Guide

See pages 90–1 of the *Teacher's Guide* for guidance on running each task. Observe children to identify those who have mastered concepts and those who require further consolidation.

★76

Oli's book has 151 pages. He has 43 more pages to read. What page is he on?

> 'More' means 'adding'.
> 151 + 43 = 194.
> You are on page 194.
> Oh no! That can't be correct as the book has only 151 pages.

What did Mia do wrong? What should the answer be?

Write 1 word problem that uses addition and numbers 151 and 43.

Now write 1 easy and 1 difficult word problem that uses:

• addition or subtraction (or both) *and*
• 3-digit numbers.

> Solve each question and show the workings clearly.

Did you know?

Addition is very important everywhere, even at London Zoo. In January each year, all the animals are lined up 2 by 2 to be counted by their keepers, then the numbers are added. They need to know this to plan the food, housing and number of people to look after them.

The ants are counted in colonies. Each colony has about 100-300 ants, so 3-digit number addition is needed!

Writing and using fractions

I wonder how many rowers there are altogether.

The number of my school bus is 100 more than the number on this bus.

Can you see tenths?

Teacher's Guide

Look at the pictures with the children and discuss the questions.
See pages 92–3 of the *Teacher's Guide* for key ideas to draw out.

79 ★

Showing numbers in different ways

You need
- Base 10 apparatus
- place-value counters
- coins

Let's learn

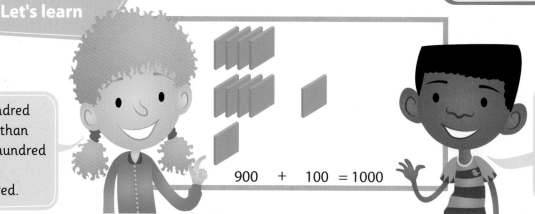

A hundred more than nine hundred is ten hundred.

$$900 \ + \ 100 = 1000$$

Yes, that's tr
It has a valu
of ten hundr
but we call i
'one thousar

Large numbers

The last 3-digit whole number is 999. When you count on 1 more you must exchange 10 ones for 1 ten.

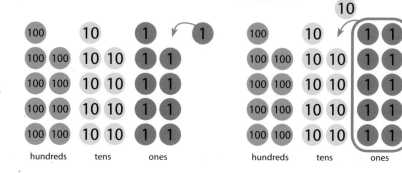

Zero is used as a place holder. The number 1000 has 1 thousand, no hundreds, no tens and no ones.

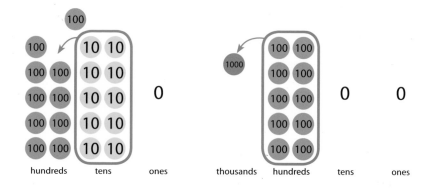

Small numbers

When an object is divided into 10 equal parts, each part is worth $\frac{1}{10}$.

Tenths are also made when you divide a single-digit number by 10, e.g.

$$1 \div 10 = \frac{1 \ \leftarrow \text{numerator}}{10 \ \leftarrow \text{denominator}} \qquad 4 \div 10 = \frac{4}{10}$$

The denominator tells you there are 10 equal parts. The numerator tells you how many of these parts there are. A fraction with a numerator 1 is called a unit fraction.

Counting on and back in fraction steps helps you to add and subtract fractions with the same denominator.

Teacher's Guide

Before working through the *Textbook*, study page 94 of the *Teacher's Guide* to see how the concepts should be introduced. Read and discuss the page with the children. Provide concrete resources to support exploration.

Make.

Copy this representation using Base 10 apparatus or place-value counters.

Find and make the numbers that are:

a   one hundred less

b   one hundred more

c   thirty more

d   two hundred less

e   one hundred and fifteen more

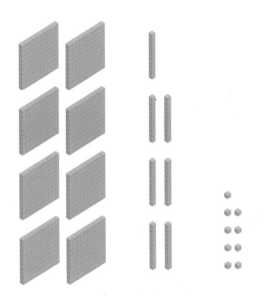

Calculate.

Use representations to prove which of these statements are true or false:

a   two more than 798 is 800

b   one hundred and one less than 1000 is 899

c   count on $\frac{3}{10}$ from $\frac{4}{10}$ to reach $\frac{8}{10}$

d   count back 5 tenths from $1\frac{1}{10}$ to reach 6 tenths

e   count on 4 tenths from 7 tenths to reach one whole.

Apply.

Here are the prices, in pence, of 4 different items at the supermarket.

a   495p

b   799p

c   825p

d   150p

If you buy 1 item at a time, work out how much change you will get from £10. Give your answers in pence.

Think.

a   Mia has 1 coin in her pocket. It is silver. Oli gives Mia $\frac{3}{10}$ of a pound. How much money could Mia have now?

b   Oli gives Mia another silver coin. She now has exactly $\frac{10}{10}$ of a pound. Find a way to make this true.

Teacher's Guide

See page 95 of the *Teacher's Guide* for ideas of how to guide practice. Work through each step together as a class to develop children's conceptual understanding.

81 ★

7b Unit and non-unit fractions

You need
- fraction bars
- paper
- ruler
- scissors

Let's learn

I have divided my strip of paper into thirds.

No, you have split it into 3 pieces but they are not equal. Thirds means 3 equal pieces.

Unit fractions

Unit fractions have a numerator with the value 1. All these shaded fractions are unit fractions.

As the size of the denominator of a unit fraction increases, the size of the actual fraction it represents decreases.

$\frac{1}{5}$ is smaller than $\frac{1}{4}$ because the whole is divided into more equal parts. The more equal parts, the smaller each part is.

To compare unit fractions, look at the denominators.

$\frac{1}{5} < \frac{1}{4}$ or $\frac{1}{4} > \frac{1}{5}$

1 ←numerator

5 ←denominator

Non-unit fractions

Non-unit fractions are all the other fractions that have a numerator that is **not** 1, e.g.:

$$\frac{3}{4} \qquad \frac{3}{10} \qquad \frac{2}{3} \qquad \frac{2}{4} \qquad \frac{3}{5}$$

$\frac{3}{5}$ of this shape is shaded red. The shape is divided into 5 equal parts. It has denominator 5 and 3 parts out of 5 parts are shaded, so 3 becomes the numerator.

To compare non-unit fractions that have the same denominator, look at the numerator. $\frac{3}{5}$ is larger than $\frac{2}{5}$ because $\frac{2}{5}$ represents 1 more of the 5 equal parts than $\frac{2}{5}$.

$\frac{2}{5} < \frac{3}{5}$ or $\frac{3}{5} > \frac{2}{5}$

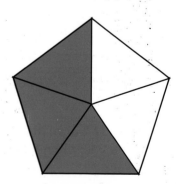

Teacher's Guide

Before working through the *Textbook*, study page 96 of the *Teacher's Guide* to see how the concepts should be introduced. Read and discuss the page with the children. Provide concrete resources to support exploration.

one whole		
$\frac{1}{3}$		
$\frac{1}{3}$		
$\frac{1}{4}$		
$\frac{1}{5}$		

Let's practise

Compare.

Think first and then use fraction bars to compare these unit fractions. Use the symbols < and > each time.

a $\frac{1}{2}$ and $\frac{1}{5}$

b $\frac{1}{5}$ and $\frac{1}{3}$

c 1 whole and $\frac{1}{2}$

d $\frac{1}{4}$ and $\frac{1}{3}$

e $\frac{1}{10}$ and $\frac{1}{5}$

f Write these unit fractions in order from smallest to largest: $\frac{1}{4}$ $\frac{1}{10}$ $\frac{1}{2}$ $\frac{1}{3}$

Answer these.

Which fractions are shown here? Write the fraction and explain to your partner how you know.

a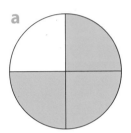
b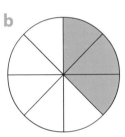
c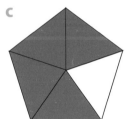
d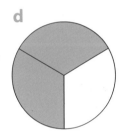
e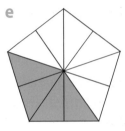

f Represent the fraction $\frac{7}{10}$ in your own way.

Apply.

Cut two 15 cm strips of paper.

Cut one strip to show $\frac{2}{3}$ and $\frac{1}{3}$. What is the length of each piece?

Use the symbols < and > to compare your fractions and record them in your book.

Now cut the other strip to show $\frac{3}{5}$ and $\frac{2}{5}$. What is the length of each piece this time?

Cut another strip of paper to your chosen length to show $\frac{3}{4}$ and $\frac{1}{4}$. Explain the choice you made.

4 Think.

Mia and Oli have some orange squash left in their glasses. Their glasses are the same size.

> I have more squash left than you, Oli!

What fraction of a glass of squash could Mia and Oli each have left?

Find as many different solutions as you can.

Teacher's Guide

See page 97 of the *Teacher's Guide* for ideas of how to guide practice. Work through each step together as a class to develop children's conceptual understanding.

83 ★

Adding and subtracting fractions

You need
- fraction bars
- number shapes or interlocking cubes
- circle shapes
- counters

Let's learn

I know that 10 tenths are equal to 1 whole so 10 quarters are also equal to 1 whole.

No, 10 quarters is more than 1 whole. When a whole is divided into quarters, there are only 4 equal parts not 10. 4 quarters are equal to 1 whole.

Fraction bonds to 1 whole

Counting on and back in fraction steps helps you to add and subtract fractions with the same denominator.

The representations show the whole as $\frac{10}{10}$ and then the fraction $\frac{3}{10}$ in yellow.

The blue part of the whole has the value of $\frac{7}{10}$.

The addition statement $\frac{3}{10} + \frac{7}{10} = 1$ describes these fractional parts.

$\frac{10}{10} = 1$

$\frac{3}{10}$

You can also use a number line and fraction bar to show the same addition.

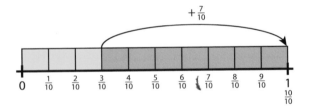

To undo the addition use the inverse subtraction statements:

$\frac{10}{10} - \frac{7}{10} = \frac{3}{10}$ or $1 - \frac{7}{10} = \frac{3}{10}$

Adding and subtracting fractions with the same denominator

Look at the representations of the addition $\frac{3}{10} + \frac{5}{10}$.

Can you see the part worth $\frac{3}{10}$ and the part worth $\frac{5}{10}$?

What is the answer to the calculation?

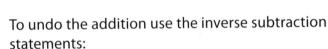

$\frac{3}{10} + \frac{5}{10} = \frac{8}{10}$

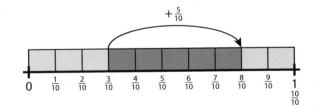

The subtraction $\frac{8}{10} - \frac{5}{10} = \frac{3}{10}$ is the inverse of the addition.

Teacher's Guide Before working through the *Textbook*, study page 98 of the *Teacher's Guide* to see how the concepts should be introduced. Read and discuss the page with the children. Provide concrete resources to support exploration.

★84

1

Copy and write.

Use number shapes or interlocking cubes cubes to copy these representations. Write the fraction addition and subtraction statement each time to show the fraction bonds to 1 whole.

a

b

c

d

e

2

Calculate.

Use fraction bars and number lines to complete these calculations:

a $\frac{2}{5} + \frac{2}{5} =$

b $\frac{4}{10} + \frac{5}{10} =$

c $\frac{7}{8} - \frac{3}{8} =$

d $\frac{4}{5} - \frac{3}{5} =$

e What calculation is shown on this fraction bar and number line?

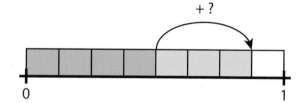

3

Apply.

Use a circle shape or fraction bar to help you answer these questions.

Write the fraction calculation each time. Give your answers as a fraction of a minute and as the number of seconds.

a $\frac{1}{2}$ a minute less than one whole minute.

b $\frac{1}{4}$ of a minute more than $\frac{2}{4}$ of a minute.

c $\frac{1}{3}$ of a minute more than $\frac{2}{3}$ of a minute.

d $\frac{1}{3}$ of a minute less than one whole minute.

e $\frac{3}{4}$ of a minute less than $\frac{4}{4}$ of a minute.

4

Think.

The answer is the fraction $\frac{3}{?}$. What is the calculation?

Find as many different addition and subtraction statements as you can that give this answer.

Teacher's Guide

See page 99 of the *Teacher's Guide* for ideas of how to guide practice. Work through each step together as a class to develop children's conceptual understanding.

85

Let's play

Player 1

Player 1

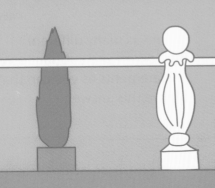

Teacher's Guide

See pages 100–1 of the *Teacher's Guide*. Explain the rules for each game and allow children to choose which to play. Encourage them to challenge themselves and practise what they have learnt in the unit.

 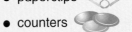
1 **Making wholes**

Spin a numerator and add counters to your gameboard to help you make a whole.

2 **Back to zero**

Spin a numerator and subtract counters from your gameboard to help you reach zero.

3 **Your game**

Design your own game using the gameboard.

And finally …

1

678 > 687
909 > 900

818 > 881
701 < 710

You need:

- Base 10 apparatus
- place-value counters
- place-value grid
- digit cards

a Use representations of your choice to check Mia and Oli's statements.

b Write all the numbers in order from smallest to largest.

2

a Use counters to show 3 different unit fractions on these shapes by covering parts. Which unit fractions are they? Explain how you know.

You need:

- counters

b Now use counters to make different non-unit fractions. Which non-unit fractions have you made? Explain how you know.

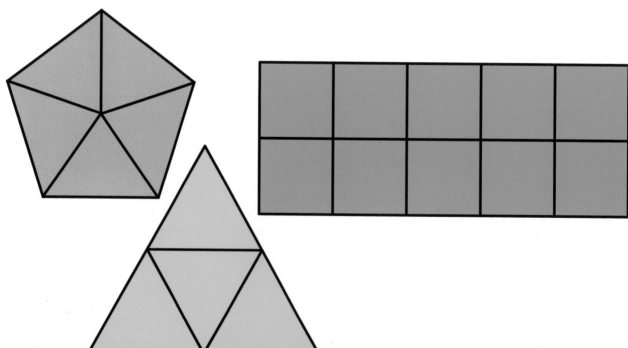

Teacher's Guide
See pages 102–3 of the *Teacher's Guide* for guidance on running each task. Observe children to identify those who have mastered concepts and those who require further consolidation.

$\frac{3}{8}$	$\frac{2}{5}$	$\frac{1}{10}$	$\frac{1}{4}$
$\frac{9}{10}$	$\frac{4}{5}$	$\frac{5}{8}$	$\frac{8}{10}$
$\frac{3}{4}$	$\frac{2}{10}$	$\frac{1}{5}$	$\frac{3}{5}$

You need:
- pencil and paper
- number shapes

a   The answer is 1. Add pairs of fractions, from the grid, that give this answer. Write the calculation you use each time.

b   Now choose different pairs of fractions to subtract. How many different answers can you make?

Did you know?

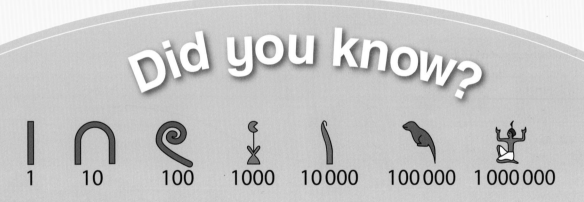

I	$\cap$	$\mathcal{C}$				
1	10	100	1000	10 000	100 000	1 000 000

...umber system is a Base 10 system, just ...e Ancient Egyptian number system. But ...yptians only had 7 different symbols ... than the 10 digits that we use. The ...ans wrote in pictures which are called ...lyphs. Their numbers were pictures too.

The picture for 1 000 000 also meant 'many'. To read or write Egyptian numbers, the largest number is always written in front of smaller numbers. The numbers are written as groups of thousands, hundreds, tens and ones. Here is the number 247, written using Egyptian hieroglyphs.

Using multiplication and division facts

I wonder what the quickest way to count the legs of all these spiders would be.

I wonder how many bags will be needed for all these apples.

How can we find out how many wheels there are on all the cars?

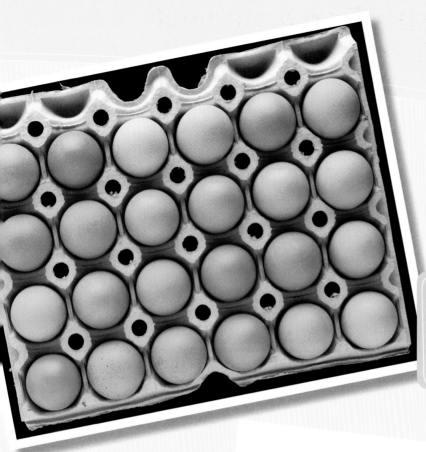

I wonder what multiplication and division facts can be made from this array of eggs.

What information can we get from this pictogram?

Year 3's favourite pets

Dog	😊 😊 😊 😊 😊
Cat	😊 😊 😊 😊 😊 😊 😊
Rabbit	😊 😊 😊 😊
Bird	😊 😊
Hamster	😊 😊
Lizard	😊

😊 = 3 children

 Teacher's Guide
Look at the pictures with the children and discuss the questions.
See pages 104–5 of the *Teacher's Guide* for key ideas to draw out.

91 ⭐

8a Multiplication tables

You need
- squared paper
- coins
- sand
- plastic bags
- scales

Let's learn

I've learnt all my multiplication facts to 6 × 12. I'm never going to remember them all the way to 12 × 12!

Don't worry – it gets easier. You don't have to learn all of them. 6 × 12 is the same as 12 × 6.

Multiplication tables

Multiplication is commutative: you do not need to learn all the multiplication facts. You only need to learn half of them! This multiplication grid goes up to 6 × 6.

×	1	2	3	4	5	6
1	1	2	3	4	5	6
2		4	6	8	10	12
3			9	12	15	18
4				16	20	24
5					25	30
6						36

Doubling and halving

Doubling is the same as multiplying by 2. Halving is the same as dividing by 2.

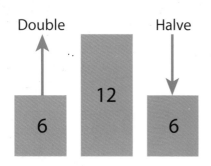

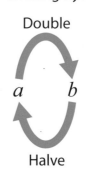

double $a = b$
half $b = a$

Doubling and halving can help you with your multiplication tables facts.

If you double and double again you are multiplying by 4. If you halve and halve again you are dividing by 4.

If you multiply by 3 and then double the answer, you are multiplying by 6.

Teacher's Guide

Before working through the *Textbook*, study page 106 of the *Teacher's Guide* to see how the concepts should be introduced. Read and discuss the page with the children. Provide concrete resources to support exploration.

Calculate.

a   Write down the multiplication facts for 4 and 8 that are commutative.

b   Write down the multiplication facts for 3 and 6 that are commutative.

Copy and complete:

c $3 \times 5 = 5 \times 3 = \boxed{}$ f $7 \times 8 = \boxed{}$

d $4 \times 9 = 9 \times \boxed{}$ g $9 \times 5 = \boxed{}$

e $6 \times 10 = 10 \times \boxed{}$ h $8 \times 6 = \boxed{}$

Calculate.

For each question, draw a doubling and halving model like this one.

Double
12   24
Halve

Double these numbers:

a   15   e   26

b   20   f   142

c   25   g   145

d   35   h   250

Halve these numbers:

i   24   m   72

j   40   n   120

k   48   o   190

l   70   p   198

Measure.

Using a set of scales, weigh each of these amounts of sand into plastic bags.

Weigh out the same amount again and add it to the bag.

What is the new mass? Write it down, then weigh it to check.

a   200 g   d   600 g

b   400 g   e   700 g

c   500 g   f.   1 kg

Think.

Oli knows all the multiplication table facts for 4 up to 12×4.

I can use these facts to make loads more!

Explain why Oli is correct.

List 20 different facts that he can make.

Explain what you have done for each one.

Teacher's Guide

See page 107 of the *Teacher's Guide* for ideas of how to guide practice. Work through each step together as a class to develop children's conceptual understanding.

93

Multiplying and dividing by 5 and 20

You need:
- place-value grids
- digit cards
- number rods
- coins

Let's learn

5 is half of 10. To multiply by 5 I can multiply by 10 and halve. To divide by 5 I can divide by 10 and halve.

You're right about multiplication. For division you have to divide by 10 and **double**, because you are dividing into half as many groups. Look at facts that you know:
$20 \div 10$ is 2, $20 \div 5$ is 4.

Multiplying by 5 and 20

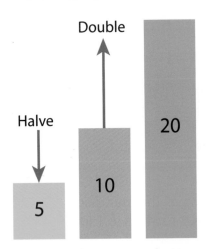

Double

Halve

20

10

5

$7 \times 20 = 140$

$7 \times 10 = 70$

$7 \times 5 = 35$

5 is half of 10, so to multiply a number by 5, multiply by 10 and halve the answer.

20 is double 10, so to multiply a number by 20, multiply by 10 and double the answer.

Dividing by 5 and 20

To divide by 5 and 20, you do the opposite of multiplying.

To divide a number by 5, divide by 10 and double the answer.

To divide a number by 20, divide by 10 and halve the answer.

$20 \div 5 = 4$

$20 \div 10 = 2$

$20 \div 20 = 1$

Teacher's Guide

Before working through the *Textbook*, study page 108 of the *Teacher's Guide* to see how the concepts should be introduced. Read and discuss the page with the children. Provide concrete resources to support exploration.

Calculate.

Multiply these numbers by 10.
Explain to a partner what is happening each time.

| a | 8 | b | 15 | c | 50 | d | 165 | e | 240 | f | 370 |

Now write an explanation.

Divide these numbers by 10.
Explain to a partner what is happening each time.

| g | 20 | h | 70 | i | 140 | j | 260 | k | 380 | l | 490 |

Now write an explanation.

Calculate.

Multiply these numbers by 5.

| a | 26 | b | 48 | c | 140 | d | 248 |

Multiply these numbers by 20.

| e | 23 | f | 57 | g | 214 | h | 257 |

Apply.

Make these amounts from coins.
Divide each amount by 5.
Make the answer using the fewest coins possible.

| a | 40p | c | £1 | e | £1.70 |
| b | 80p | d | £1.50 | f | £2.30 |

Make these amounts from coins.
Divide each amount by 20.
Make the answer using the fewest coins possible.

| g | 20p | i | £1.40 | k | £2.20 |
| h | 60p | j | £1.80 | l | £3.60 |

Think.

4

I multiplied my number by 20 and then divided it by 5. I ended up with 96. What was my number?

Find Mia's number. Explain how you know.

Make up some of your own 'What's my number?' problems to give to a partner to solve.

Teacher's Guide

See page 109 of the *Teacher's Guide* for ideas of how to guide practice.
Work through each step together as a class to develop children's conceptual understanding.

95 ★

Missing number problems and scaling

Let's learn

If I am given a problem like 8 × ▢ = 24, I have to divide 24 by 8 to get the missing number.

You could do that. If you do you are using the inverse. You can also count on in 8s to find out how many you need to make 24.

Missing number problems

To solve 8 × ▢ = 24, work out 24 ÷ 8 = 3.

Or count on in 8s to find out how many you need to make 24: 8, 16, 24.

So the missing number is 3.

You can use a diagram like this to help you:

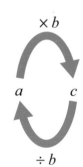

$a \times b = c$
$b \times a = c$
$c \div b = a$
$c \div a = b$

Scaling up and scaling down

You can scale up to make something bigger and scale down to make something smaller.

When you scale up you multiply.

When you scale down you divide. Scaling down involves finding a fraction of the amount.

Twice as big

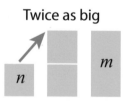

$\frac{1}{2}$ of the size

Three times as big

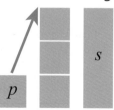

$\frac{1}{3}$ of the size

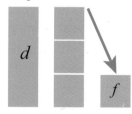

Teacher's Guide

Before working through the *Textbook*, study page 110 of the *Teacher's Guide* to see how the concepts should be introduced. Read and discuss the page with the children. Provide concrete resources to support exploration.

1

Calculate.

Find the missing number in each of these statements.

a $\boxed{} \times 3 = 27$ c $7 \times \boxed{} = 56$ e $15 \div \boxed{} = 3$

b $6 \times \boxed{} = 24$ d $\boxed{} \div 4 = 8$ f $\boxed{} \div 8 = 6$

Explain to a partner how you found the missing numbers.

2

Calculate.

Scale these amounts up so they are 3 times the size.
For each, draw a scaling diagram to show what you did.

a 12   b 15   c 21   d 50

Scale these amounts down so they are $\frac{1}{4}$ the size.
For each, draw a scaling diagram to show what you did.

e 24   f 48   g 100   h 160

3

Apply.

Measure and cut out strips of paper to each of these lengths.

a 2 cm   c 8 cm   e 15 cm

b 3 cm   d 10 cm   f 25 cm

Scale each length up so that they are 4 times the length.
Cut strips of paper to show the new lengths.
You may have to stick pieces together!

Now scale each of the original lengths down so that they are half the length.
Cut strips of paper to show the new lengths.

4

Think.

Oli scaled a whole number up. His product was 64

What was my starting number? What did I scale up by?

Find as many possible solutions as you can.

Teacher's Guide

See page 111 of the *Teacher's Guide* for ideas of how to guide practice. Work through each step together as a class to develop children's conceptual understanding.

97 ★

High fives!

Let's play

Start

Teacher's Guide
See pages 112–13 of the *Teacher's Guide*. Explain the rules for each game and allow children to choose which to play. Encourage them to challenge themselves and practise what they have learnt in the unit.

 5 and 20

Multiply by 5 and 20 to win points.

 Higher and lower

Scale the amounts up and down to score points.

 Your game

Make up your own game using the gameboard.

99 ⭐

And finally ...

Let's review

1

Look at this multiplication grid. All the products are missing.
Copy the grid onto squared paper.
Write in all the facts that you need to know in order to complete it.

You need:
- squared paper

Explain why you only need to write in half of the facts.
Now explain why this will not work for division.

×	1	2	3	4	5	6	7	8	9	10	11	12
1												
2												
3												
4												
5												
6												
7												
8												
9												
10												
11												
12												

2

Solve these missing number problems.
For each one, draw a diagram to show your thinking.

You need:
- counters (optional)

a $\boxed{} \times 3 = 33$

b $6 \times \boxed{} = 48$

c $7 \times \boxed{} = 28$

d $\boxed{} \times 10 = 90$

$\times b$

$a \qquad c$

$\div b$

e $36 \div \boxed{} = 12$

f $\boxed{} \div 4 = 20$

g $\boxed{} \div 5 = 7$

h $21 \div \boxed{} = 7$

Teacher's Guide   See pages 114–15 of the *Teacher's Guide* for guidance on running each task.
Observe children to identify those who have mastered concepts and those who
require further consolidation.

a Multiply these numbers by 5 and 20. Use the strategies you have been learning about:

24 48 62 45 54

b Divide these numbers by 5 and 20. Use the strategies you have been learning about.

40 60 90 120 150

c Make the number 10 four times bigger.
Draw a scaling up diagram to show this.
Now write a multiplication statement for the calculation.

d Make the number 32 a quarter of the size.
Draw a scaling down diagram to show this.
Now write a division statement for the calculation.

e Choose a number of your own. Scale it up by 3 different amounts.
Choose another number. Scale it down by 3 different amounts.

Do this again for another pair of numbers.
And again!

Be careful which number you choose to scale down!

Did you know?

eople often use scaling
o and down in real life.
ook at this map. It has
een scaled down.

To work out the actual distances we need to scale them back up.

0 20 km

Exploring lines and turns

I wonder why the train tracks never cross each other.

I wonder what angle the black bars make with the red ones.

How far does the wheel need to turn before you reach the top of London Eye?

I wonder which way the children should turn to face each other.

I wonder how I could describe the line between the sea and the sky.

These buildings stand upright and very tall! I wonder how we could describe this.

Teacher's Guide

Look at the pictures with the children and discuss the questions.
See pages 116–17 of the *Teacher's Guide* for key ideas to draw out.

103 ★

Let's learn

These lines will never meet each other. They are parallel lines.

No, that's wrong! **Parallel lines** are lines that never meet no matter how long they are extended.

Not parallel lines

Parallel lines

Perpendicular lines

2 lines that meet at right angles are perpendicular lines.

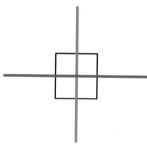

Horizontal lines

Horizontal lines are lines that are parallel to the floor. Lines A to B and D to C are horizontal lines.

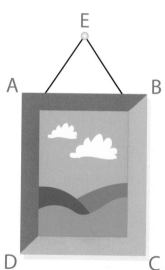

Floor

Vertical lines

Vertical lines make right angles with horizontal lines. Lines AD and BC are vertical lines.

Teacher's Guide

Before working through the *Textbook*, study page 118 of the *Teacher's Guide* to see how the concepts should be introduced. Read and discuss the page with the children. Provide concrete resources to support exploration.

Answer these.

1 2 3 4

a   List the lines that are parallel.

b   List the lines that are perpendicular.

Identify.

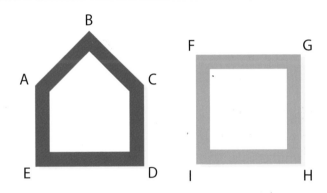

a   List 4 horizontal and
     vertical lines.

b   List 2 pairs of perpendicular
     and parallel lines.

Apply.

Use modelling clay to make:

a   A shape that has no
     parallel lines.

b   A shape that has
     horizontal and
     vertical lines.

c   A shape that
     has parallel and
     perpendicular lines.

Think.

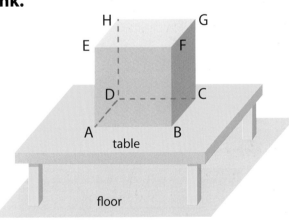

Place a box in the shape of a cuboid on your table.

Are there more sets of parallel or perpendicular lines
in the box?

Teacher's Guide

See page 119 of the *Teacher's Guide* for ideas of how to guide practice.
Work through each step together as a class to develop children's
conceptual understanding.

105

9b Turning

Let's learn

The second cuboid is bigger than the first one because it's taller.

No, they are the same cuboids! If you turn the first cuboid 1 right angl clockwise, you'll get the second one.

Turns

The ⬆ needs to turn 1 right angle clockwise to land on the ➡.

This is a **quarter turn**. It is 1 right angle turn clockwise.

The ⬆ needs to turn 2 right angles clockwise to land on the ⬇.

This is a **half turn**.

The arrow turned 2 right angles clockwise. What direction will the arrow face if it turns 2 right angles anticlockwise?

The ⬆ needs to turn 3 right angles clockwise to land on the ⬅.

This is a **three-quarter turn**.

The ⬆ can also turn 1 right angle anticlockwise to land on the ⬅.

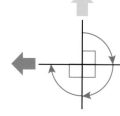

4 right angles clockwise make a **full turn**. The will land on the same place it started. What happens if the turns are anticlockwise?

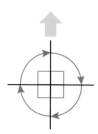

Turning patterns

Patterns can be made by turning a shape.

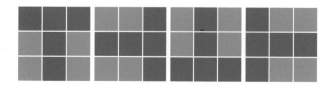

This pattern is made from turning the T shape a $\frac{1}{4}$ turn.

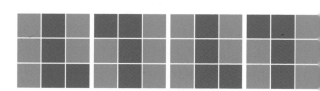

This pattern is made from turning the L shape a $\frac{1}{2}$ turn.

Teacher's Guide

Before working through the *Textbook*, study page 120 of the *Teacher's Guide* to see how the concepts should be introduced. Read and discuss the page with the children. Provide concrete resources to support exploration.

Describe.

Describe the turns needed and their direction to move from one shape to the other.

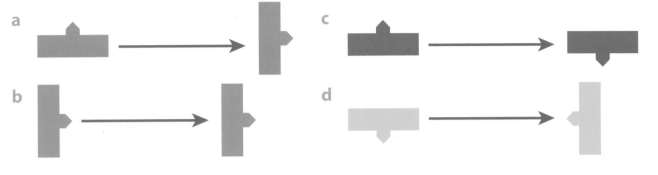

a

b

c

d

Answer these.

a Copy the table and complete each turn.

Start at	Turn	End at
▲	$\frac{1}{2}$ turn clockwise	
▼	$\frac{1}{4}$ turn clockwise	
▶	$\frac{3}{4}$ turn clockwise	
◀	$\frac{3}{4}$ turn clockwise	

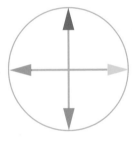

b Copy and complete the table.

Start at	Turn	End at
▶		▼
▼		▲
▲		◀
◀		▼

Apply.

Work in pairs. Choose a shape, e.g. a triangle. Make a repeating pattern by turning the shape 5 times clockwise at right angle turns and drawing around the shape at each position. Your partner describes the rule used and predicts the next 2 shapes in the pattern.

Think.

Copy, complete and describe the way the shape is being turned. Can you think of a different way?

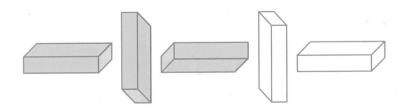

Teacher's Guide

See page 121 of the *Teacher's Guide* for ideas of how to guide practice.
Work through each step together as a class to develop children's
conceptual understanding.

107 ★

Lines and turns

Let's play

Start

Teacher's Guide

See pages 122–3 of the *Teacher's Guide*. Explain the rules for each game and allow children to choose which to play. Encourage them to challenge themselves and practise what they have learnt in the unit.

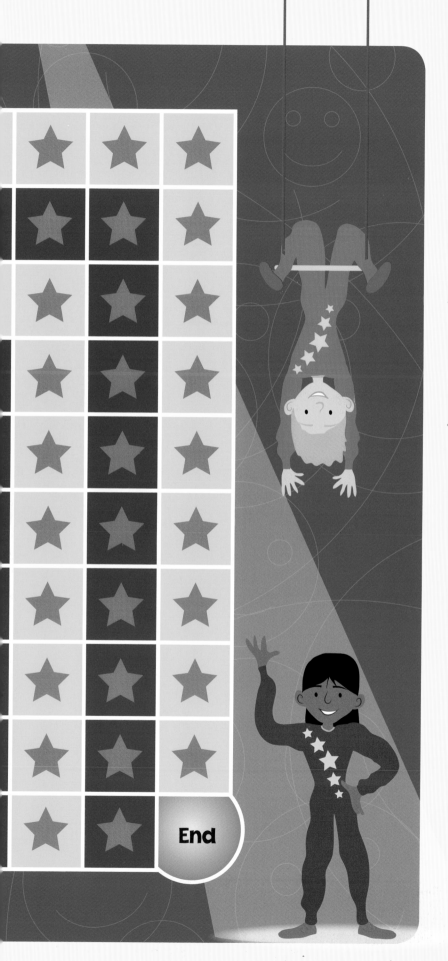

1 **Horizontally or vertically?**

Move horizontally or vertically to reach the end. Who will get there first?

2 **Keep turning!**

Turn at right angles to reach the end. Who will get there first?

3 **Your game**

Make up your own game using the gameboard.

End

109

And finally ...

Let's review

1

Work in 2 groups: the parallel and perpendicular group.

Use different colours to draw as many pairs of parallel and perpendicular lines as you can.

The winning group is the one that has drawn the most pairs of lines.

You need:
- dotted paper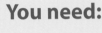
- coloured pencils

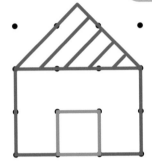

> I drew a house by using parallel and perpendicular lines. Can you spot them?

2

Look at this turning pattern. Spot the mistake.
Now, draw the correct pattern and describe its rule.

You need:
- squared paper
- ruler

Teacher's Guide

See pages 124–5 of the *Teacher's Guide* for guidance on running each task. Observe children to identify those who have mastered concepts and those who require further consolidation.

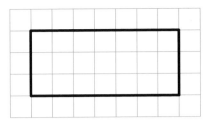

You need:
- squared paper
- ruler

Draw a rectangle. Insert horizontal or vertical lines only that would cut the rectangle into 4 equal parts.
How many ways can you find?

Did you know?

...he world's ...opulation is growing ...o fast that planners ...re now thinking ...bout building ...ertical cities!

Wow! We will have to take vertical roads that go up and down to go to the school, park or cinema!

Using number and place value

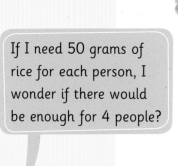

If I need 50 grams of rice for each person, I wonder if there would be enough for 4 people?

20:00 New York	183	Will depart B gates
20:05 Aberdeen	1318	Gate shown 19:15
20:05 Glasgow	5975	Gate shown 19:15
20:10 Cape Town	5949	Gate shown 18:55
20:15 Dubai	105	Will depart B gates
20:15 Nice	352	Gate shown 19:25
20:15 Stockholm	4788	Gate shown 19:25
20:15 Munich	7165	Gate shown 19:25
20:25 Newcastle	1338	Gate shown 19:35
20:50 Johannesburg	057	Gate shown 19:45

I wonder which is the largest number in this departure board?

What fraction of the digits on this keypad is on the top row?

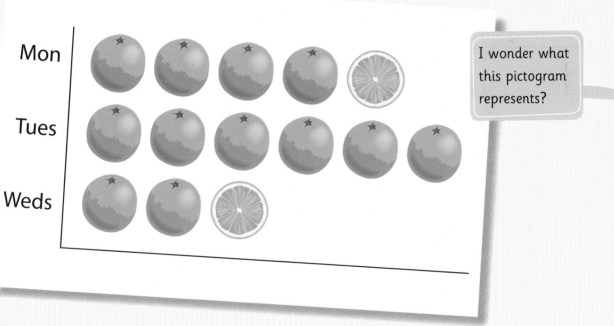

Mon

Tues

Weds

I wonder what this pictogram represents?

Teacher's Guide

Look at the pictures with the children and discuss the questions.
See pages 126–7 of the *Teacher's Guide* for key ideas to draw out.

113 ★

Reading and writing numbers

Let's learn

 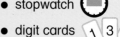
I write the number 570 in words as five hundred and seventeen.

No, 70 is seven tens. You write it as five hundred and seventy.

Numerals and words

Numbers can be written in numerals and words.

Look at the words that represent each part of these numbers.

The word 'and' helps you to read the numbers clearly.

684 → | 600 | 80 | 4 | six hundred and eighty-four

680 → | 600 | 80 | | six hundred and eighty

604 → | 600 | | 4 | six hundred and four

In 604 a zero is used to hold the tens place. It tells you there are no tens in the number.

Reading and writing numbers as time

You count in steps of 5 to read the minutes around a clock face.

Digital times are shown as the number of minutes after the hour.

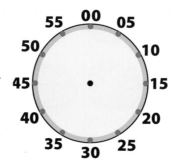

| 9:25 | 11:40 |
| 8:09 | 5:31 |

The o'clock position is shown as 00. The 5-past position is shown as 05.

The minutes always have 2 digits on a digital clock.

To read the top 2 digital times you say *nine twenty-five* and *eleven forty*.

To read these on an analogue clock you say, *twenty-five past nine* and *twenty to twelve*.

a.m. shows morning (before midday)

p.m. shows afternoon (after midday or noon).

Midday is 12:00 p.m.

Midnight is 12:00 a.m. as it starts a new day.

Teacher's Guide

Before working through the *Textbook*, study page 128 of the *Teacher's Guide* to see how the concepts should be introduced. Read and discuss the page with the children. Provide concrete resources to support exploration.

Write.

Write each number in numerals.

a   four hundred and
    ninety-nine

b   eight hundred and six

c   nine hundred and
    seventeen

Write each number in words.

d   512   e   780   f   263   g   305

Write.

Write each time
as a digital time
in numbers and
in words.

Remember to
write a.m. or p.m.

a   morning   b   afternoon   c   morning   d   noon

Estimate.

Estimate how many hops you can do or
how far you can count from zero in the
times given.

Use a stop watch to time your activity.
How close to your estimate were you
each time?

> Remember that
> there are 60
> seconds in a minute.

a   forty-five seconds

b   sixty seconds

c   one hundred and twenty seconds

Think.

Mia and Oli each make some 3-digit
numbers. They compare them.
Oli's numbers **always** have 8 hundreds.
Mia's numbers **always** have 8 ones.

> My number will
> be larger than
> Mia's number!

Find out if Oli's statement is always
true, sometimes true or never true.

Teacher's Guide

See page 129 of the *Teacher's Guide* for ideas of how to guide practice.
Work through each step together as a class to develop children's
conceptual understanding.

115 ⭐

Using place value

Let's learn

Double five is ten, so double fifty is ten-hundred.

No! Double 5 tens is 10 tens, which is equal to 100.

Ten times larger

Number rods represent the numbers 1 to 10.

You can give the rods new values by multiplying each number by 10. Use place value to help.

The orange rod has been multiplied by 10.
It now has the value 100. It is 10 times larger than 10.

The yellow rod is half the length of the orange rod.
It has the value 50 because it is 10 times larger than 5.

The relationship between 8 and 4 and 80 and 40 works in the same way.

Here, each representation is equivalent.
They all have a total value of 200.

| 100 | 50 |
| 80 | 40 |

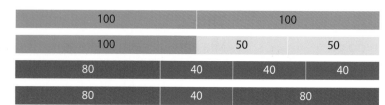

$200 = 100 + 100$

$200 = 100 + 50 + 50$

$200 = 80 + 40 + 40 + 40$

$200 = 80 + 40 + 80$

Ten times smaller

You can divide shapes, objects and numbers by 10. Each equal part is worth $\frac{1}{10}$.
Each part is 10 times smaller than the whole.

Here there are 3 wholes. When you divide each one by 10, you get $\frac{3}{10}$ altogether:

$$\frac{1}{10} + \frac{1}{10} + \frac{1}{10} = \frac{3}{10}$$

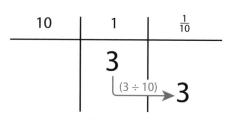

Teacher's Guide

Before working through the *Textbook*, study page 130 of the *Teacher's Guide* to see how the concepts should be introduced. Read and discuss the page with the children. Provide concrete resources to support exploration.

Calculate.

Copy these representations. Write the total value each time.

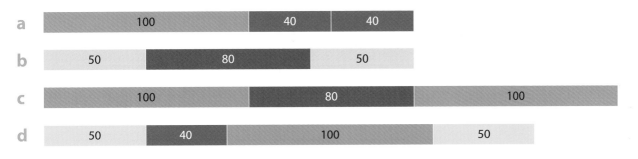

a | 100 | 40 | 40 |

b | 50 | 80 | 50 |

c | 100 | 80 | 100 |

d | 50 | 40 | 100 | 50 |

Answer these.

Use the same number rods. Make 2 different representations for each number.

a 350

b 280

c 250

d 340

Now write 2 statements for each number to show how it is partitioned.

Start with 350 =

Apply.

Use digit cards and a place-value grid to show how each fraction is made.

Write the division statement you use each time.

a $\frac{5}{10}$ c $\frac{9}{10}$

b $\frac{2}{10}$ d $\frac{7}{10}$

Now count in steps of $\frac{2}{10}$ to 2. Write the fractions in your count.

Think.

Look at the bar chart. It shows the number of seconds it took each player to find the first child in a game of 'Hide and seek'.

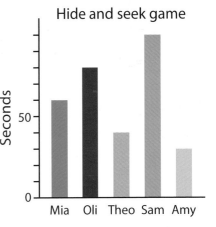

Hide and seek game

Use the scale to find and compare each time.

Write a statement to show what you have found out.

Now write another. And another.

How many different statements can you write?

Teacher's Guide
See page 131 of the *Teacher's Guide* for ideas of how to guide practice.
Work through each step together as a class to develop children's
conceptual understanding.

117 ⭐

Time travel

 **End**

| + 1 min | + 8 mins | | + $\frac{3}{4}$ hr | − 75 min |

| + 1 hr | + 60 mins | | + $\frac{1}{4}$ hr | − 35 mi |

| + 30 mins | | − 25 mins | + 90 mins | |

| | + 5 mins | + $\frac{3}{4}$ hr | − 10 mins | |

|  | | | | |

| + 45 mins | − 5 mins | | + 10 mins | |

Start 6:00 a.m. | + 5 mins | | + 10 mins | + 15 mins | + 5 mi |

Teacher's Guide

See pages 132–3 of the *Teacher's Guide*. Explain the rules for each game and allow children to choose which to play. Encourage them to challenge themselves and practise what they have learnt in the unit.

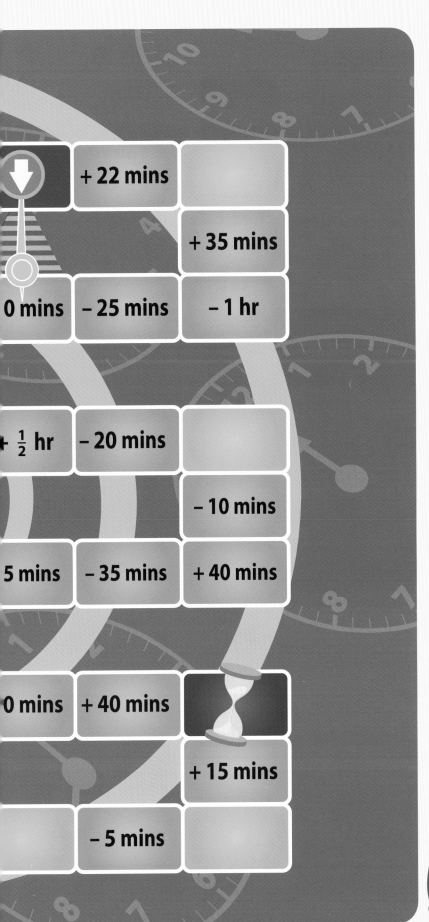

+ 22 mins

+ 35 mins

0 mins   **– 25 mins**   **– 1 hr**

+ $\frac{1}{2}$ hr   **– 20 mins**

– 10 mins

5 mins   **– 35 mins**   **+ 40 mins**

0 mins   **+ 40 mins**

+ 15 mins

– 5 mins

 1 Beat the clock

Add and subtract minutes and hours as you race round the track. Who will have the earlier time at the end?

 2 It's nearly noon!

Think carefully about the number of spaces you move! The winner has a time that is nearer to noon.

 3 Your game

Design your own game using the gameboard. Explain the rules and play with a partner.

Let's review

1

Use these words to make as many different numbers as you can.

Read each number. Show it with digit cards.

How many different numbers can you make?

You need:

- digit cards

	forty	
six hundred		one
	seventy	
three hundred		eight
	twenty	
nine hundred		five
	ten	

2

Show an o'clock time on your clock face.
Decide if the time is in the morning or afternoon.
Write it as a digital time.

You need:

- clocks

Follow these instructions:

Move the hands on your clock.
Write each time as a digital time.

Show the time that is:
- $\frac{3}{4}$ hour earlier
- 20 minutes earlier than your new time
- 120 minutes later than your new time
- 12 minutes earlier than your new time.

What is the time now?

Teacher's Guide

See pages 134–5 of the *Teacher's Guide* for guidance on running each task.
Observe children to identify those who have mastered concepts and those who require further consolidation.

Start with 5 wholes.

Roll the dice. Count back this number of tenths.

Record the count as you go.

1	$\frac{1}{10}$

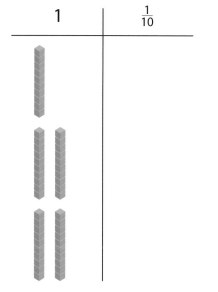

What is the last step you need to count back to reach zero?

Did you know?

...used to use the sun to tell the ...sing a sundial! Numbered lines ...ent each hour of daylight. As the ...ppears to move across the sky, ...s a shadow on the dial plate. ...n tell the time by looking at the ...n of the shadow.

The ancient Egyptians made the earliest known sundial in about 3500 BCE. This was made from a stick or pillar that cast a shadow on the ground. The ancient Greeks also made sundials. Clocks began to replace sundials in the 1300s.

3-digit sums and differences

What could you buy with the money?

£1.99

£8.99

£2.8

99p

£2.80

99p

Is the sum of the numbers on each row on the left bigger than the numbers on the right?

If the game ends at 10.45am, I wonder how many minutes there are until the end?

Number of snowy days

North Pole	❄	❄	❄	❄
Scotland	❄			
Russia	❄	❄	❄	
England	❄			

Key: ❄ = 100 snowy days

How many more days did it snow in the North Pole than in England?

Teacher's Guide

Look at the pictures with the children and discuss the questions.
See pages 136–7 of the *Teacher's Guide* for key ideas to draw out.

123

Adding 3-digit numbers

I used column addition to find 103 + 406 = 59.

That's not correct. The sum can't be less than the numbers you're adding. The zero is missing from your answer. It has no tens in it.

Mental methods of addition

A mental method of addition can be used to calculate 465 + 323.

Partition the numbers:

- Add the ones: $5 + 3 = 8$
- Add the tens: $60 + 20 = 80$
- Add the hundreds: $400 + 300 = 700$
- Then add together: $700 + 80 + 8 = 788$

Use subtraction to check the answer.

If $465 + 323 = 788$, then $788 - 465 = 323$ and $788 - 323 = 465$.

100	10	1
4	6	5
+ 3	2	3

Formal written method of addition

Use the column method of addition to work out 367 + 529:

Add the ones.

Add the tens.

Add the hundreds.

$7 + 9 = 16$ so carry 1 ten into the tens column.

```
  100 10  1
    3  6  7
 +  5  2  9
    8  9  6
       1
```

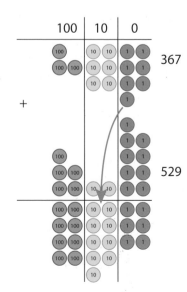

Teacher's Guide

Before working through the *Textbook*, study page 138 of the *Teacher's Guide* to see how the concepts should be introduced. Read and discuss the page with the children. Provide concrete resources to support exploration.

Explain to your partner how your mental method works.

Calculate.

Add these numbers mentally.

a   530 + 430 =

c   453 + 524 =

e   301 + 248 =

b   460 + 460 =

d   540 + 307 =

f   350 + 450 =

Calculate.

Choose a mental or written method.

Remember to make an estimate first.

a   134 + 147 =

c   238 + 142 =

e   523 + 228 =

b   465 + 216 =

d   569 + 319 =

f   519 + 377 =

Apply.

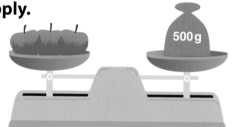

3 apples weigh about 500 grams.

Pick up 2 items in your classroom that you think weigh less than 500 grams.

Measure the weight of each item separately.

Calculate the total amount of the 2 items. Estimate first.

Did you use a mental or written method?

Now measure again with 2 different items.

Think.

132	346	120
620	371	350
252	319	101

Choose 2 numbers. Add them to make:

a   the largest sum possible

b   the smallest sum possible

c   the largest odd number possible

d   the smallest even number possible.

Teacher's Guide

See page 139 of the *Teacher's Guide* for ideas of how to guide practice. Work through each step together as a class to develop children's conceptual understanding.

125 ★

Subtracting 3-digit numbers

Let's learn

I used column subtraction to find 945 – 937 = 12. I subtracted the smaller numbers from the larger ones.

$$\begin{array}{r} 945 \\ -\ 937 \\ \hline 12 \end{array}$$

That's not right! 945 – 937 = 8, because 45 – 37 = 8. You could check by using a number line or counting on.

Mental methods of subtraction

When subtracting, see if you can use a mental method first.

To calculate 350 – 199, you can subtract the nearest multiple of 100 and add the extra ones you have subtracted.

350 – 200 = 150, 100 + 1 = 151.

350 – 199 can also be shown using a bar model.

Then use counting up on the number line to find the difference.

Use the addition 199 + 151 = 350 to check the answer.

350		
199		?

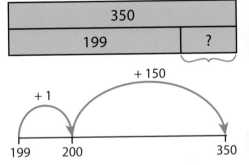

+ 150

+ 1

199   200   350

Formal written method of subtraction

To solve 463 –125 a written method is needed.

In the ones column, you can not calculate 3 – 5 because there are not enough ones to subtract 5.

One of the tens has to move into the ones column to become ten ones. You can then complete the calculation.

Use the addition 338 + 125 = 463 to check the answer.

100	10	1
400	60	3

$$\begin{array}{r} {\scriptstyle 100\ \ 10\ \ 1} \\ 4\ 6\ 3 \\ -\ 1\ 2\ 5 \\ \hline \end{array}$$

100	10	1
400	50	13

$$\begin{array}{r} {\scriptstyle 100\ \ \ 10\ \ \ 1} \\ 4\ {\scriptstyle 5}6\ {\scriptstyle 1}3 \\ -\ 1\ 2\ 5 \\ \hline 3\ 3\ 8 \end{array}$$

Teacher's Guide   Before working through the *Textbook*, study page 140 of the *Teacher's Guide* to see how the concepts should be introduced. Read and discuss the page with the children. Provide concrete resources to support exploration.

★126

Calculate.

Complete these calculations. Make an estimate first.

a   480 − 250 =

b   750 − 299 =

c   202 − 198 =

d   830 − 110 =

e   690 − 370 =

f   776 − 759 =

g   Write the addition calculations you would use to check your answers.

> Will you use a mental or written method? Why?

Calculate.

Choose a mental or written method. Remember to estimate first.

a   774 − 108 =

b   580 − 349 =

c   671 − 348 =

d   754 − 247 =

e   671 cm − 349 cm =

f   482 kg − 325 kg =

g   653 ml − 239 ml =

h   £751 − £232 =

> For questions e to h, make up word problems to match each calculation.

Apply.

You are selling stationery items in the Year 3 shop. All the prices are more than £1, e.g. £1.70, £1.34, £1.01, £2.99. All the children have more than £1 but less than £10 to spend.

Take it in turn to buy and sell. Calculate the change.

Use a mental or written method. Write down the calculations clearly.

Repeat with 5 items. How many different subtractions can you make?

Think.

> I am thinking of two 3-digit numbers. The first number is the largest 3-digit number possible that starts with 7. The second number is the smallest 3-digit number possible that ends with 2.

What is the difference between the 2 numbers Mia is thinking of?

acher's Guide

See page 141 of the *Teacher's Guide* for ideas of how to guide practice. Work through each step together as a class to develop children's conceptual understanding.

127

Add-venture take-away pizza

Let's play

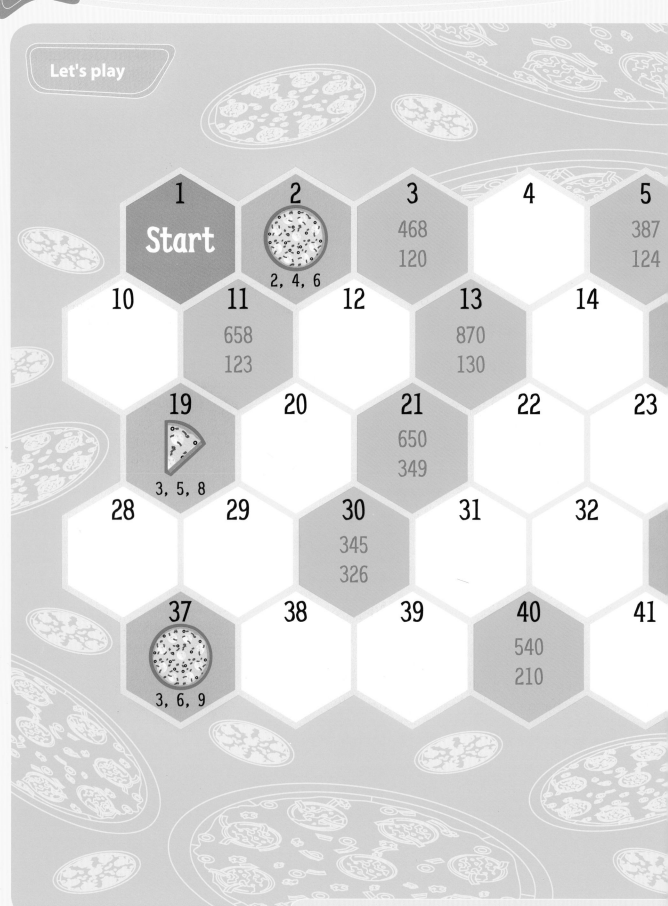

1

Start

2

2, 4, 6

3

468

120

4

5

387

124

10

11

658

123

12

13

870

130

14

19

3, 5, 8

20

21

650

349

22

23

28

29

30

345

326

31

32

37

3, 6, 9

38

39

40

540

210

41

Teacher's Guide

See pages 142–3 of the *Teacher's Guide*. Explain the rules for each game and allow children to choose which to play. Encourage them to challenge themselves and practise what they have learnt in the unit.

1 **Pizza additions**

Add numbers to collect points. See who can collect the most!

2 **Take-away pizza**

Subtract numbers to collect points. Who will collect the most?

3 **Your game**

Make up your own game using the gameboard. Explain the rules and play with a partner.

And finally ...

1

There are 375 lizards and 125 snakes in the Sahara Park. How many more lizards than snakes are there?

Oli does the calculation 375 + 125.
Mia does the calculation 375 − 125.

Who is correct?
Explain how you know.

Copy and complete the diagram.
Find the total number of lizards and snakes.

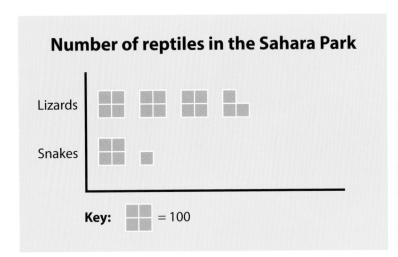

Number of reptiles in the Sahara Park

Lizards

Snakes

Key: = 100

2

I am thinking of a number. I add 123 to it. My answer is 378. What was my number?
I am thinking of another number. I subtract 130 from it. My answer is 250. What was my number?

Now it is your turn.
Make 1 easy and 1 difficult question for your partner.

If the answer is 120, what could the question be?

Does your partner need to add or subtract?

Teacher's Guide
See pages 144–5 of the *Teacher's Guide* for guidance on running each task. Observe children to identify those who have mastered concepts and those who require further consolidation.

Copy the grids. Use the column method of addition to find the sum of the rows and columns.

228	315	
116	239	

168	229	
326	567	

Use the column method of addition and subtraction to find the missing numbers.

?	216	?
225	?	891
764	982	

Make 1 easy and 1 difficult addition and subtraction grid for your friend. How can you check they are correct?

Did you know?

ition is important everywhere, even n making bubbles! You pour 100 ml of hing-up liquid into a 1 litre jar, then 600 ml of warm water. Sprinkle on oon of sugar. Slowly stir the solution 700 ml of bubbles are mixed together.

You need addition for home-made snow too! Take 10 sheets of kitchen towels (150 grams) and cut them into small pieces using a food mixer. **Add** 750 g of baking soda to a bowl. **Add** 1 tablespoon of water at a time while mixing. Do you think there is more or less than 1 kg of 'snow' in the bowl?

12 Representing whole numbers and fractions

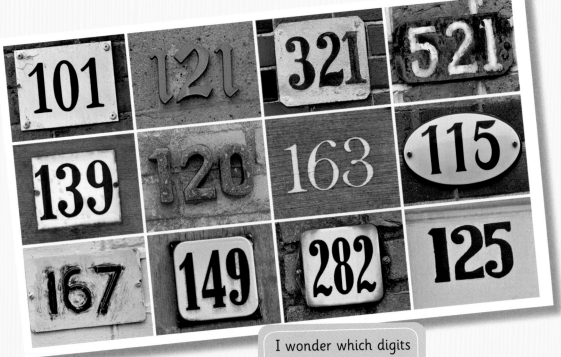

I wonder which digits have been used to show hundreds, tens and ones?

How many pennies are there?

How many different ways can I share my bottle of orange squash equally?

I can see some different fractions here! Can you?

Teacher's Guide
Look at the pictures with the children and discuss the questions.
See pages 146–7 of the *Teacher's Guide* for key ideas to draw out.

133 ★

12a Representing whole numbers and tenths

Let's learn

A whole always has a value of 1.

Sometimes! A 'whole' can also represent a larger group, for example, a whole class of children.

You need
- ten frames or squared paper
- counters
- cubes
- ruler and pencils
- bead string

Representing whole numbers

These 3 ten frames represent a 3-digit whole number.
Each frame has a value of hundreds, tens or ones.

The number is made up of 3 hundreds, 6 tens and 9 ones or 300 + 60 + 9 = 369.

These frames represent 369 in different ways.

All 3 representations have an equivalent value, even though they do not all look the same.

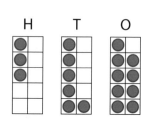

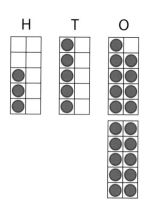

$$369 = 300 + 50 + 19 \qquad 369 = 200 + 160 + 9$$

Representing tenths

Here the same ten frame is used to represent 10 tenths.
The whole is divided by 10 to make 10 equal parts.
You write this as $\frac{10}{10}$.

This bead string is also divided into 10 equal parts to represent tenths, but there are more than 10 beads altogether.

Each tenth is made up of 10 beads, so $\frac{10}{10}$ or 1 whole is made up of 100 beads.

Teacher's Guide

Before working through the *Textbook*, study page 148 of the *Teacher's Guide* to see how the concepts should be introduced. Read and discuss the page with the children. Provide concrete resources to support exploration.

1 Calculate.

	H	T	O
	●		
	●	●	
	●	●	
	●●	●●	●
	●●	●	●●

a What is the value of this representation?

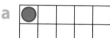 + + =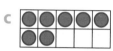

b Use ten frames and counters to show the number in different ways using partitioning.
Write a number statement each time.

2 Calculate.

What fraction does each ten frame represent?

a ●☐☐☐☐ ☐☐☐☐☐   **b** ●●●● ☐   **c** ●●●●● / ●●

Count the number of tenths in each row.

What is the value of each row?

d ●●●● ☐   ●●●●● ☐   ●●●●● / ●

e ●●●●● / ●●   ●●●●● / ●●●   ●●

3 Measure.

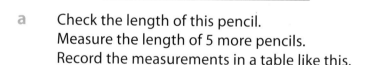

a Check the length of this pencil.
Measure the length of 5 more pencils.
Record the measurements in a table like this.

Pencil	Whole (centimetres)	Tenths (of a centimetre)
1	7	$\frac{3}{10}$

b How can you represent 7 wholes and 3 tenths on a bead string?

4 Think.

a Set out a row of 10 cubes. If this is the whole, how many cubes equal $\frac{1}{10}$?
Add another row. If the 2 rows are the whole, how many cubes equal $\frac{1}{10}$?
Add another row. If the 3 rows are the whole, how many cubes equal $\frac{1}{10}$?

b What can you say about the number of cubes each time that equal $\frac{5}{10}$?

What patterns do you notice?

Teacher's Guide
See page 149 of the *Teacher's Guide* for ideas of how to guide practice.
Work through each step together as a class to develop children's conceptual understanding.

135 ★

Finding and using unit and non-unit fractions

Let's learn

$\frac{3}{10}$ is a unit fraction because the numerator is a single-digit number.

No, that's not right. All unit fractions have 1 as the numerator, so $\frac{3}{10}$ is a non-unit fraction.

Unit and non-unit fractions

Fractions are numbers on the number line.

$\frac{1}{5}$ and $\frac{1}{8}$ are unit fractions because they have numerators of 1.

$\frac{3}{5}$ and $\frac{5}{8}$ are non-unit fractions as their numerators are not 1. $\frac{3}{5}$ has the same value as 3 steps or lots of $\frac{1}{5}$.

You can use number lines and fraction bars to compare fractions.

$\frac{1}{5} > \frac{1}{8}$ because the same whole is divided into only 5 equal parts rather than 8 equal parts.

$\frac{3}{5} > \frac{1}{5}$ because $\frac{3}{5}$ is the same as 3 lots of $\frac{1}{5}$.

$\frac{5}{8} > \frac{1}{8}$ because $\frac{5}{8}$ is the same as 5 lots of $\frac{1}{8}$.

Unit fractions as operators

Using unit fractions as operators is linked to dividing.

Finding a half of an object or a group of objects is the same as dividing by 2.

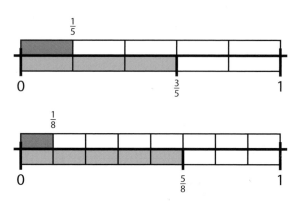

For a group of 20 objects, you can say that $\frac{1}{2}$ of 20 is 10 or $20 \div 2 = 10$.

These fraction bars represent $\frac{1}{4}$ of 20 or the division statement $20 \div 4$.

The answer to both calculations is the same, 5.

20			
$\frac{1}{4}$			

Teacher's Guide

Before working through the *Textbook*, study page 150 of the *Teacher's Guide* to see how the concepts should be introduced. Read and discuss the page with the children. Provide concrete resources to support exploration.

Compare.

Use fraction bars and a number line to compare these pairs of fractions.
Record your findings using < or >.

a $\frac{1}{5}$ and $\frac{1}{10}$ b $\frac{3}{10}$ and $\frac{7}{10}$ c $\frac{1}{3}$ and $\frac{1}{4}$ d $\frac{4}{5}$ and $\frac{1}{5}$

e   Write the fractions $\frac{1}{5}$, $\frac{1}{10}$, $\frac{4}{5}$ and $\frac{3}{5}$ in order from smallest to largest.

f   Write the fractions $\frac{1}{4}$, $\frac{1}{3}$, $\frac{1}{5}$ and $\frac{3}{4}$ in order from largest to smallest.

Answer these.

Write a fraction statement and a division statement for each of these representations.
Calculate each answer.

a
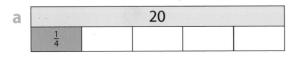

c
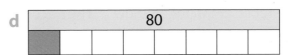

b

d

e   Use fraction bars to represent the division 25 ÷ 5. What is the matching fraction statement?

4

Apply.

Draw a 12 cm line to represent 1 whole. Label it from zero to 1.

Show the fractions $\frac{1}{4}$, $\frac{2}{4}$, $\frac{3}{4}$ and $\frac{4}{4}$ on the line.

Now draw another 12 cm line and show the fractions $\frac{1}{3}$, $\frac{2}{3}$ and $\frac{3}{3}$.

What other fractions can you show?

Think.

Mia and Oli each count out a different number of 50p coins.

$\frac{1}{10}$ of my coins is 50p.

$\frac{1}{8}$ of my coins is 50p.

a   How much money does each child have?

b   What other fractions of amounts could 50p represent? Investigate to come up with at least 5 more examples.

Teacher's Guide

See page 151 of the *Teacher's Guide* for ideas of how to guide practice.
Work through each step together as a class to develop children's
conceptual understanding.

137 ★

12c Equivalent fractions

You need
- fraction bars
- counters
- number lines

Let's learn

I waited $\frac{2}{4}$ of an hour for the bus yesterday!

You usually say '$\frac{1}{2}$ an hour', but it has the same value as $\frac{2}{4}$ of an hour.

Equivalent fractions

2 fractions or a group of fractions are equivalent when they have the same value.

They represent the same fraction of a whole, but they do not look the same.

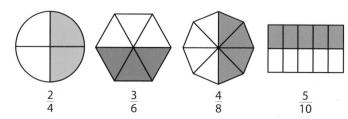

$\frac{2}{4}$ $\frac{3}{6}$ $\frac{4}{8}$ $\frac{5}{10}$

These representations all show $\frac{1}{2}$. The fractions look different each time, but the numerator is always half the value of the denominator.

Equivalent fractions also share the same position on a number line.

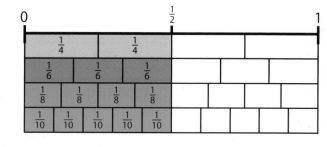

You can write this string of equivalent fractions as $\frac{1}{2} = \frac{2}{4} = \frac{3}{6} = \frac{4}{8} = \frac{5}{10}$.

Adding and subtracting fractions

You can add and subtract fractions that share the same denominator.

These fraction bars and number lines show the calculations $\frac{5}{8} + \frac{1}{8} = \frac{6}{8}$ and $\frac{7}{8} - \frac{3}{8} = \frac{4}{8}$.

You can write the answers as equivalent fractions with lower denominators.

$\frac{6}{8}$ is equivalent to $\frac{3}{4}$ and $\frac{4}{8}$ is equivalent to $\frac{1}{2}$.

So $\frac{5}{8} + \frac{1}{8} = \frac{6}{8}$ or $\frac{3}{4}$ and $\frac{7}{8} - \frac{3}{8} = \frac{4}{8}$ or $\frac{1}{2}$.

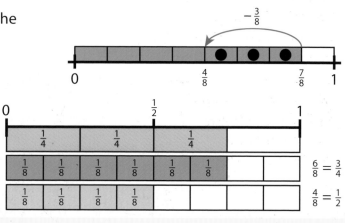

$\frac{6}{8} = \frac{3}{4}$

$\frac{4}{8} = \frac{1}{2}$

Teacher's Guide

Before working through the *Textbook*, study page 152 of the *Teacher's Guide* to see how the concepts should be introduced. Read and discuss the page with the children. Provide concrete resources to support exploration.

Answer these.

Which pairs of fractions are equivalent? Use fraction bars to help you.

a $\frac{3}{10}$ and $\frac{2}{5}$ = ☐

b $\frac{2}{4}$ and $\frac{5}{10}$ = ☐

c $\frac{1}{5}$ and $\frac{2}{10}$ = ☐

d $\frac{7}{8}$ and $\frac{3}{4}$ = ☐

e $\frac{1}{3}$ and $\frac{2}{6}$ = ☐

f $\frac{3}{8}$ and $\frac{1}{4}$ = ☐

g Now write the pairs of equivalent fractions you found using the equals (=) sign, e.g. $\frac{1}{2} = \frac{2}{4}$.

Calculate.

Complete these addition and subtraction calculations.

a $\frac{3}{5} + \frac{2}{5}$ = ☐

b $\frac{4}{5} - \frac{3}{5}$ = ☐

c $\frac{9}{10} - \frac{4}{10}$ = ☐

d $\frac{7}{8} - \frac{1}{8}$ = ☐

e $\frac{1}{10} + \frac{3}{10}$ = ☐

f $\frac{2}{6} + \frac{2}{6}$ = ☐

g $1 - \frac{1}{4} - \frac{1}{4}$ = ☐

h $\frac{5}{10} + \frac{2}{10}$ = ☐

i Look for any answers where an equivalent fraction can be written with a lower denominator.

Apply.

Mia and Oli are running races on separate tracks.

Use counters and fraction bars to represent the children and the tracks.

Find out what fractions of the track they can each run so they are always equal in the race.

Use other fraction bars to represent different tracks.

How many different equivalent fractions can you find?

Think.

Oli and Mia have lots of each of these weights:

$\frac{1}{10}$ kg, $\frac{1}{5}$ kg, $\frac{1}{4}$ kg, $\frac{1}{8}$ kg.

They want to measure exactly $\frac{1}{2}$ kg of flour on their balancing scales.

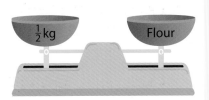

Write calculations to show all the different ways that you can measure exactly $\frac{1}{2}$ kg.

What other masses of ingredients can you measure? Show how you know.

Teacher's Guide

See page 153 of the *Teacher's Guide* for ideas of how to guide practice. Work through each step together as a class to develop children's conceptual understanding.

139 ⭐

Fraction action!

Let's play

$\frac{1}{4}$	$\frac{2}{4}$	$\frac{6}{8}$
$\frac{4}{5}$	$\frac{1}{2}$	$\frac{2}{3}$

$\frac{6}{8}$	$\frac{4}{6}$	$\frac{2}{10}$
$\frac{3}{5}$	$\frac{3}{4}$	$\frac{1}{2}$

$\frac{3}{6}$	$\frac{1}{5}$	$\frac{3}{4}$
$\frac{1}{4}$	$\frac{4}{8}$	$\frac{1}{3}$
$\frac{1}{2}$	1	$\frac{5}{10}$

$\frac{1}{4}$	$\frac{5}{10}$	$\frac{3}{5}$
$\frac{4}{10}$	$\frac{5}{5}$	$\frac{1}{3}$

$\frac{2}{6}$	1	$\frac{1}{5}$
$\frac{1}{4}$	$\frac{6}{10}$	$\frac{2}{3}$

Teacher's Guide — See pages 154–5 of the *Teacher's Guide*. Explain the rules for each game and allow children to choose which to play. Encourage them to challenge themselves and practise what they have learnt in the unit.

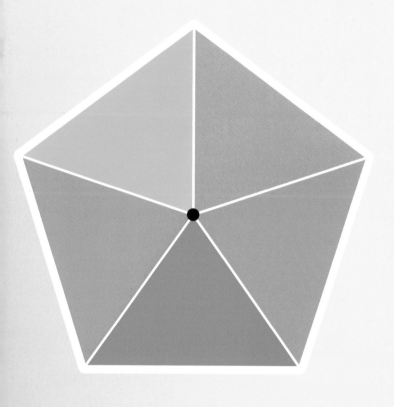

1 3 in a row

Score points by completing a row of 3 fractions. Who will have the most points at the end?

2 Making pairs

Find pairs of equivalent fractions and cover both with a counter. The player who finishes with the most counters on the gameboard is the winner.

3 Your game

Design your own game. Explain the rules and play with a partner.

Let's review

1

You need:
- digit cards 0-9
- Base 10 apparatus
- place-value counters and/or ten frames

Use 3 digit cards each time to make a 3-digit number.

Show the number using manipulatives or a drawing.

Rearrange the digits to make another number and then another.

Order the 3 numbers, starting with the smallest.

2

Oli and I made equivalent fraction pairs.
Here is what we found out.

You need:
- fraction bars
- counters
- number lines

$$\frac{4}{8} = \frac{2}{4} \qquad \frac{3}{4} = \frac{7}{8}$$

$$\frac{1}{2} = \frac{5}{10} \qquad \frac{1}{5} = \frac{3}{10}$$

$$\frac{1}{3} = \frac{3}{6} \qquad \frac{2}{8} = \frac{1}{4}$$

Mark the children's work using fraction bars or a method of your choice.

Teacher's Guide
See pages 156–7 of the *Teacher's Guide* for guidance on running each task. Observe children to identify those who have mastered concepts and those who require further consolidation.

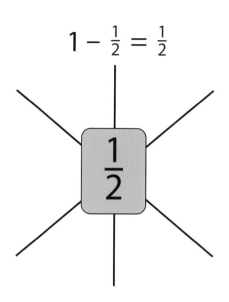

$$1 - \frac{1}{2} = \frac{1}{2}$$

Make up the story of a $\frac{1}{2}$ using as many addition and subtraction calculations as you can. Each has to have an answer of a $\frac{1}{2}$. One has been done for you.

Remember that there are many fractions with different denominators that are equivalent to a half!

You can add extra legs to the story so you can write more calculations.

Did you know?

...e we used centimetres and metres for ...uring, we used units called inches and feet. ... were other larger units too like yards and miles. ... people still use these units of measurement ... United Kingdom and in the United States of ...ica. Many carpenters still use fractions of an ...when they measure lengths of wood.

If you look at rulers and tape measures, you will often see inches on them. An inch is divided into equal parts so measurements can be more accurate. On this tape measure you can see quarters, eighths and the fraction $\frac{1}{2}$. Some of the eighths are not labelled because they are equivalent to quarters.

Written methods for multiplication and division

I wonder how many seedlings there are altogether?

How much would it cost to buy 5 cartons?

How can I find out how many squares are on this chessboard?

How much would 1 courgette cost?

4 for 96p

I wonder how much money I have altogether?

Teacher's Guide

Look at the pictures with the children and discuss the questions.
See pages 158–9 of the *Teacher's Guide* for key ideas to draw out.

145 ★

13a Towards the written method for multiplication

Let's learn

To multiply 34 by 3, I could add 34, 3 times couldn't I?

You could, but there is a quicker way. You could use a written method.

Array to grid method

The array shows 34×3. The second diagram shows the answer, 102.

You can write 34×3 in a grid.

Partition the multiplicand into tens and ones. Multiply each part by the multiplier. Then add the results together, $90 + 12 = 102$. So $34 \times 3 = 102$.

When you add each part and exchange you get 102.

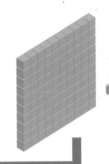

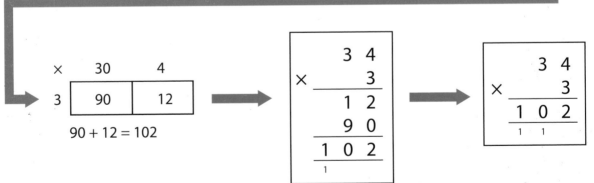

×	30	4
3	90	12

$90 + 12 = 102$

$$\begin{array}{r} 3\ 4 \\ \times \quad 3 \\ \hline 1\ 2 \\ 9\ 0 \\ \hline 1\ 0\ 2 \\ \hline \scriptstyle 1 \end{array}$$

$$\begin{array}{r} 3\ 4 \\ \times \quad 3 \\ \hline 1\ 0\ 2 \\ \scriptstyle 1 \quad 1 \end{array}$$

Grid to formal written method

You can also use a written method.

Multiply the ones by the multiplier, then the tens.

Then add the results together, so $34 \times 3 = 102$.

Teacher's Guide

Before working through the *Textbook*, study page 160 of the *Teacher's Guide* to see how the concepts should be introduced. Read and discuss the page with the children. Provide concrete resources to support exploration.

★146

Calculate.

Use Base 10 apparatus to make an array for each calculation.
Record your information in a grid.

a   45 × 3

b   35 × 6

c   32 × 8

d   65 × 3

Don't forget to work out the answer!

Calculate.

Work out the answers to these multiplications.
For each, use the grid and both written methods.

a   31 × 6

b   27 × 3

c   43 × 7

d   24 × 8

Apply.

Make an array for each of these calculations. Use £1, 10p and 1p coins.
Show your information in a grid.

a   24p × 3   e   24p × 6

b   53p × 3   f   53p × 6

c   62p × 3   g   62p × 6

d   93p × 3   h   93p × 6

Compare the products of the amounts you multiplied by 3 with the products of the amounts you multiplied by 6. What do you notice?

Remember to work out the product of each.

4 Think.

What are the missing numbers in these calculations?

a
$$
\begin{array}{r}
\blacksquare\,4 \\
\times\quad 3 \\
\hline
\blacksquare\,0\ 2 \\
\end{array}
$$

b
$$
\begin{array}{r}
2\,\blacksquare \\
\times\quad 3 \\
\hline
\blacksquare\,8 \\
\end{array}
$$

c
$$
\begin{array}{r}
1\,\blacksquare \\
\times\quad 3 \\
\hline
\blacksquare\,1 \\
\end{array}
$$

d
$$
\begin{array}{r}
\blacksquare\,\blacksquare \\
\times\quad 3 \\
\hline
\blacksquare\,3\ 5 \\
\end{array}
$$

Explain how you worked out the missing numbers.

Make up some missing number calculations like these for your partner to solve.

Teacher's Guide

See page 161 of the *Teacher's Guide* for ideas of how to guide practice.
Work through each step together as a class to develop children's conceptual understanding.

147

Towards the written method for division

Let's learn

To divide 72 by 3, I could take away 3 lots of times, couldn't I?

You could, but that would take a long time. You could take away multiples of 3, or you could use a written method.

Arrays for division

These arrays show $8 \times 4 = 32$ and $4 \times 8 = 32$.

You can also use arrays to find the inverse division calculations.

$32 \div 8 = 4$ and $32 \div 4 = 8$.

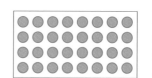

Partitioning and the formal written method

Here is one way to work out $72 \div 3$:

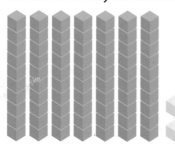

Partition 72 into 60 and 12.
$60 \div 3 = 20$ and $12 \div 3 = 4$.
So $72 \div 3 = 24$.

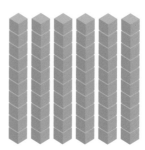

Here is another way:

Find how many groups of 3 tens you can make.

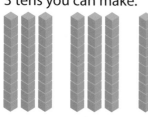

There are 2.

$$3 \overline{\smash{)}7\ 2} \quad ^2$$

Exchange the remaining ten for ones.

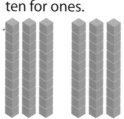

$$3 \overline{\smash{)}7\ {}^12} \quad ^2$$

Find out how many groups of 3 ones you can make.

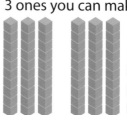

There are 4.

$$3 \overline{\smash{)}7\ {}^12} \quad ^{2\ 4}$$

Teacher's Guide

Before working through the *Textbook*, study page 162 of the *Teacher's Guide* to see how the concepts should be introduced. Read and discuss the page with the children. Provide concrete resources to support exploration.

Make your arrays using counters or cut them out from squared paper.

Calculate.

Make an array for each calculation.

Write down the division calculation that your array shows.

a   6 × 3   c   15 × 3   e   8 × 6

b   12 × 3   d   4 × 6   f   12 × 6

Calculate.

Use partitioning and facts that you know to answer these.

Check your answers using the written method.

a   78 ÷ 3   e   96 ÷ 6   i   108 ÷ 3

b   78 ÷ 6   f   96 ÷ 8   j   108 ÷ 12

c   96 ÷ 3   g   108 ÷ 9

d   96 ÷ 4   h   108 ÷ 6

Apply.

Use the formal written method to answer these.

Model each calculation using 10p and 1p coins.

a   72p ÷ 3   f   84p ÷ 7

b   72p ÷ 6   g   78p ÷ 3

c   52p ÷ 4   h   87p ÷ 3

d   96p ÷ 4   i   54p ÷ 9

e   96p ÷ 8   j   68p ÷ 4

4

Think.

I made some arrays with 48 counters. I wrote down all the multiplication and inverse division calculations that I could make.

Work with a partner.

Use 48 counters to make as many arrays as you can.

Write down all the possible calculations Oli could have made.

Have you found all the possibilities?

Explain how you know to another pair.

Teacher's Guide

See page 163 of the *Teacher's Guide* for ideas of how to guide practice.
Work through each step together as a class to develop children's
conceptual understanding.

149 ⭐

Seeing stars

Let's play

3 6 8

2 6 5

4 6 3

5 6 8

Teacher's Guide

See pages 164–5 of the *Teacher's Guide*. Explain the rules for each game and allow children to choose which to play. Encourage them to challenge themselves and practise what they have learnt in the unit.

1 **Cosmic multiplication**

Multiply numbers to earn counters. Get 3 counters in a row to win.

2 **Intergalactic division**

Divide numbers to earn counters. Get 3 counters in a row to win.

3 **Your game**

Make up your own game using the gameboard.

Let's review

1

a   Write down the multiplication that this array shows. Use Base 10 apparatus to find the answer.

b   Show how you can answer the calculation using the grid method. Do you get the same answer?

c   Do the calculation using the expanded and then the formal written methods.

d   Which method do you prefer? Explain why.

2

Look at the diagrams. They look like arrays with the middle missing! They also look like the formal written method for division.

a

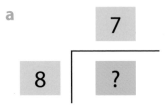

 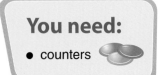
Work out the missing numbers.

Explain how you did this to your partner.

For each diagram, write down the 4 number statements that you can make.

b   12 / 4 = ?

c   5 / 9 = ?

d   8 / 6 = ?

e   15 / 3 = ?

Teacher's Guide

See pages 166–7 of the *Teacher's Guide* for guidance on running each task. Observe children to identify those who have mastered concepts and those who require further consolidation.

Answer these division questions by partitioning.
The first one is done for you.

You need:
- Base 10 apparatus

a   51 ÷ 3

 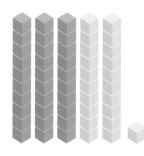

You can partition 51 into 30 and 21.
You know that $10 \times 3 = 30$ and $7 \times 3 = 21$, so the answer is $10 + 7 = 17$.

b   92 ÷ 4   c   78 ÷ 6   d   87 ÷ 3   e   91 ÷ 7

Answer these using the formal written method.

f   56 ÷ 4   g   84 ÷ 7   h   72 ÷ 6   i   76 ÷ 4

Did you know?

…e formal written methods we …e for addition, subtraction, …ultiplication and division are …amples of algorithms.

An algorithm is a sequence of instructions that are followed step by step. The word 'algorithm' comes from the Latin form of the name of the 9th century Persian scientist, astronomer and mathematician Abdullah Muhammad ibn Musa al-Khwarizmi.

2-D shapes and perimeter

I like the shape of this hedge. It makes a pentagon.

This parachute is made from 12 triangles!

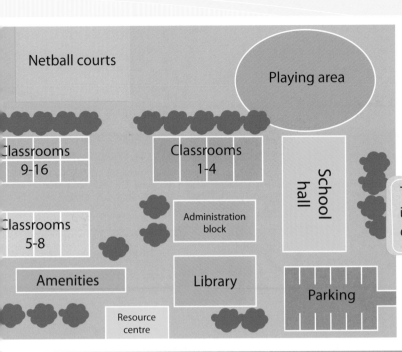

This school map is made from lots of shapes!

How can I find out how far the children are cycling?

100 metres

I wonder whether the pink or the blue ribbon is longer.

Teacher's Guide

Look at the pictures with the children and discuss the questions.
See pages 168–9 of the *Teacher's Guide* for key ideas to draw out.

155

All about 2-D shapes

You need
- 2-D shapes
- squared paper
- ruler
- coloured pencils
- scissors

Let's learn

5 cm on this square seems very short!

5 cm

It's just an illustration. It's not an exact measurement. Illustrations can show the length the shapes should be.

Describing 2-D shapes

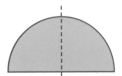

This is a semicircle. It has 1 straight and 1 curved side. It has a vertical line of symmetry.

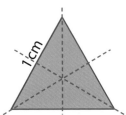

This triangle has equal sides. They are all 1 cm long. It has 3 lines of symmetry.

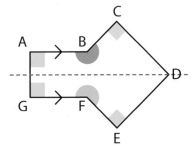

This shape has 7 sides and 7 vertices. It is a **heptagon**. It has 4 right angles and a line of symmetry.

This is a **composite** shape. It is formed by 2 shapes: a triangle and a rectangle.

Drawing 2-D shapes

There are many ways to draw 2-D shapes, e.g.:

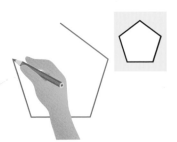

Copy a shape carefully.

Draw around an object.

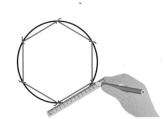

Draw a circle. Mark 6 points on the circle and then join the dots using a ruler.
How many dots would you need to draw a pentagon?

Teacher's Guide

Before working through the *Textbook*, study page 170 of the *Teacher's Guide* to see how the concepts should be introduced. Read and discuss the page with the children. Provide concrete resources to support exploration.

Name and draw.

Name these shapes.

Explain your reasoning.

Draw them on squared paper.

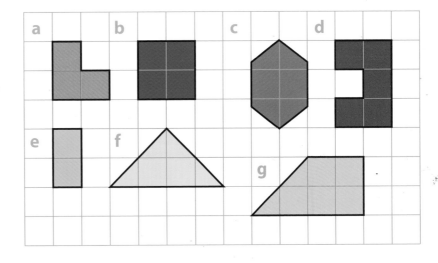

Draw.

Using squared paper, draw:

a   a rectangle with sides of 3 cm and 2 cm

b   a heptagon

c   2 different hexagons

d   a 2-D shape of your choice.

Design.

Work in pairs.

Join up to ten 2-D shapes together to make an object e.g.:

- boat
- train
- robot
- pet.

Draw the object and cut it out.

Your partner must describe the shapes you use and the object you make.

Take turns.

4 Think.

Draw a square.

Inside the square draw a rectangle.

What is different between your 2 shapes?

Teacher's Guide

See page 171 of the *Teacher's Guide* for ideas of how to guide practice.
Work through each step together as a class to develop children's
conceptual understanding.

157 ★

Measuring perimeter

Let's learn

The total length around this square is 4 because it has 4 squares in it.

1 cm

No. This square has 4 sides. Each side is 2 squares or 2 cm long. The total length is 2 cm + 2 cm + 2 cm + 2 cm or 4 × 2 cm = 8 cm.

How to measure perimeter

The total length around a shape is called the perimeter.

To find the perimeter add the lengths of all the sides of the shape.

Perimeter of regular, irregular and compound shapes

Regular shapes

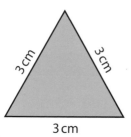

3 cm, 3 cm, 3 cm

Perimeter = 3 cm + 3 cm + 3 cm = 9 cm = 90 mm

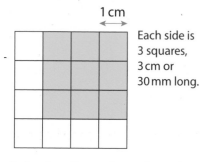

1 cm

Each side is 3 squares, 3 cm or 30 mm long.

Perimeter = 3 cm + 3 cm + 3 cm + 3 cm = 12 cm = 120 mm

Irregular shapes

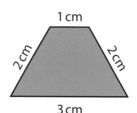

1 cm, 2 cm, 2 cm, 3 cm

Perimeter = 1 cm + 2 cm + 3 cm + 2 cm = 8 cm = 80 mm

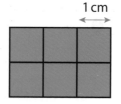

1 cm

This rectangle is 3 cm wide and 2 cm long.

Perimeter = 3 cm + 2 cm + 3 cm + 2 cm = 10 cm = 100 mm

Compound shapes

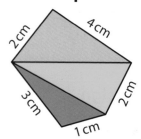

2 cm, 4 cm, 3 cm, 2 cm, 1 cm

Perimeter = 4 cm + 2 cm + 1 cm + 3 cm + 2 cm = 12 cm = 120 mm

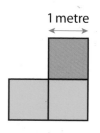

1 metre

Perimeter = 8 m = 800 cm

Teacher's Guide

Before working through the *Textbook*, study page 172 of the *Teacher's Guide* to see how the concepts should be introduced. Read and discuss the page with the children. Provide concrete resources to support exploration.

Measure.

Use a ruler to measure the sides of each shape.

Find the perimeter of each shape.

Which shape has the smallest perimeter?

Which has the biggest?

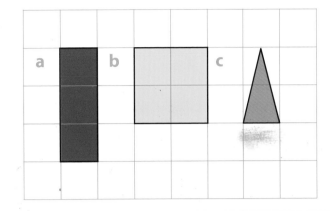

Calculate.

Name each shape. Find the perimeter.

Copy and complete the table below.

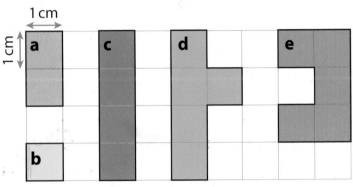

	Polygons with 4 sides or less	Polygons with more than 4 sides
Perimeter less than 8 cm		
Perimeter 8 cm or more		

How much longer is the perimeter of the blue rectangle than that of the orange square?

Draw.

Work in a small group.

Draw 6 different shapes on the playground.

Use chalk or washable paint.

Each shape must have a perimeter of 1 m 20 cm.

Describe the shapes.

What is different between them?

Think.

Look at this table.

All the shapes are regular and have sides of 2 cm each.

Number of sides of the regular shape	3	4	5	6	7	8
Perimeter in centimetres						

a　Copy and complete the table. Is there a pattern?

b　What would the perimeter of a 10-sided shape be?

c　How much shorter is the perimeter of a triangle than that of an octagon in the pattern?

Teacher's Guide

See page 173 of the *Teacher's Guide* for ideas of how to guide practice. Work through each step together as a class to develop children's conceptual understanding.

159 ★

Black or white?

Let's play

Teacher's Guide

See pages 174–5 of the *Teacher's Guide*. Explain the rules for each game and allow children to choose which to play. Encourage them to challenge themselves and practise what they have learnt in the unit.

You need:

- 1-6 dice
- counters
- squared paper
- rulers

1 **Odd one out**

Name shapes and decide on the odd one out to win points!

2 **Guess my shape!**

Ask questions to guess the shape your partner is thinking of!

3 **Your game**

Make up your own game using the gameboard. Explain the rules and play with a partner.

And finally ...

Work in pairs.
Use a 4 × 4 dotted grid.

Each draw a quadrilateral with the longest possible perimeter.

Measure the lengths. Compare the results with your partner.

Repeat for:

a   triangle

b   pentagon

c   hexagon

d   octagon.

You need:

- dotted paper
- colouring pencils
- ruler

The winner is the one who has drawn the shapes with the biggest perimeter!

Look at these shapes.

Which shapes do not have a perimeter of 10 cm?

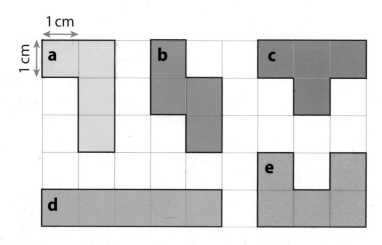

You need:

- ruler
- colouring pencils
- squared paper

Teacher's Guide

See pages 176–7 of the *Teacher's Guide* for guidance on running each task. Observe children to identify those who have mastered concepts and those who require further consolidation.

3 Copy these shapes in a square grid:

a   A square with 3 cm sides. Label it A.

b   A square smaller than A. Label it B.

c   A triangle that has a right angle and 2 shorter sides of length 2 cm.

d   A rectangle with horizontal sides of 6 cm and vertical sides of 2 cm.

e   Cut the shapes out. Explore the different pentagons, hexagons and octagons you can make. Draw round and label your shapes.

You need:
- squared paper
- ruler
- colouring pencils
- scissors

Does your shape have a line of symmetry?

Did you know?

One of the longest running races in the world is 5000 km or 5 000 000 m long. It takes 6–10 weeks to complete and is held in New York. Runners run 5649 laps around a city block with a perimeter of 900 metres!

One of the shortest fun runs in the world is held in Burntwood, England. People run around a small triangle park with a perimeter of 50 metres. It takes about 10 seconds to complete. That is a challenge!

⭐3 Glossary

2-dimensional (2-D)

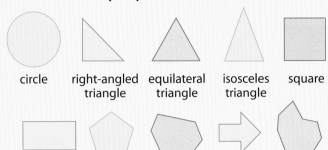

circle   right-angled   equilateral   isosceles   square
          triangle   triangle   triangle

rectangle   pentagon   hexagon   heptagon   octagon

3-dimensional (3-D)

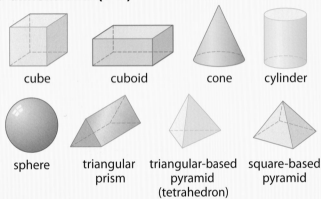

cube   cuboid   cone   cylinder

sphere   triangular   triangular-based   square-based
          prism   pyramid   pyramid
                        (tetrahedron)

5, 10, 15 ... minutes past

Ways of counting minutes on an analogue clock. The minute hand takes 5 minutes to move between each hour mark on the clock face. See also *analogue clock*.

12-hour time

Counting hours of the day in 2 blocks of twelve. 12.01-12 noon as a.m. and 12.01-12 midnight as p.m. Often told on a 12-hour clock with hands and known as analogue time.

24-hour time

Counting hours of the day from 0-24. Used on digital clocks. 2 p.m. is written as 14:00.

A

acute angle

An angle between 0° and 90°. See also *obtuse, reflex angle*.

addend

The number being added in an addition calculation. Augend + addend = sum (or total).

addition

A mathematical operation combining 2 or more numbers to find a total. Augend + addend = sum (or total).

$$3 + 5 = 8$$

augend   addend   sum/total

a.m.

From Latin ante-meridian, meaning before midday. See also *12-hour time*.

analogue clock

A dial with hands used to show time. The dial shows 12 hours in a full circle. The minute hand moves 1 complete turn every circle.

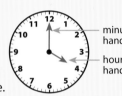

minute hand

hour hand

angle

The amount of turn between 2 straight lines that meet at a point. Usually measured in degrees. Symbol: °. See also *acute, obtuse, reflex angle*.

approximate, approximately

A number that is not exact, e.g. 2028 is approximately 2000. Symbol: ≈.

array

An arrangement of numbers, shapes or objects in rows of equal size and columns of equal size, used to find out how many altogether.

column

row

$12 \times 3 = 36$

augend

The number being added to in an addition calculation. Augend + addend = sum (or total)

$$3 + 5 = 8$$

augend   addend   sum/total

axis, axes

Horizontal and vertical lines on a graph.

B

balance

Things are balanced when both sides have equal value, e.g. 3 + 4 = 7 and 1000 g = 1 kg.

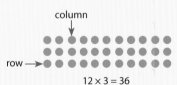

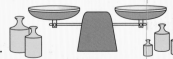

bar chart

A chart drawn using rectangular bars to show how large each value is.

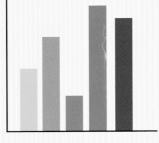

base

The flat surface under a 3-D shape, e.g. a square-based pyramid has 1 square base and 4 triangular faces.

C

calendar

A list of the days of the year, arranged by month, week and day.

capacity

The amount a container holds. It is measured in litres or millilitres, e.g. the capacity of a 2-litre bottle is 2 litres.

Carroll diagram

A Carroll diagram sorts objects according to a criteria and not that criteria. There can be 2 different criteria but always the criteria and not the criteria, e.g. odd numbers/not odd numbers, multiples of 5/not multiples of 5, dogs/not dogs.

	odd	not odd
< 50	23	18
not < 50	57	92

Celsius

A scale used to measure temperature. Sometimes called Centigrade. Units are °C.

centimetre

A unit of length, 1 metre = 100 centimetres. Symbol: cm.

century

100 years.

commutative

Addition and multiplication are commutative. It does not matter which way you add, or multiply the answer is always the same. Same answer, different calculation, e.g. 3 + 4 = 4 + 3, 3 × 4 = 4 × 3. But subtraction and division are not commutative, e.g. 7 − 2 ≠ 2 − 7, 6 ÷ 2 ≠ 2 ÷ 6.

D

degree

A unit of temperature. °C for degrees Celsius, though Centigrade is often still used.

denominator

The number of parts the whole has been divided into. The number underneath the vinculum. Also called the divisor. See also *numerator*.

diagram

A sketch or accurate drawing of a mathematical shape or problem.

difference

The result of a subtraction. The difference between 12 and 5 is 7. See also *minuend, subtrahend*.

digit

The symbols 0, 1, 2, 3, 4, 5, 6, 7, 8 and 9. The value of each digit depends on its position, e.g. in 16, the digit 1 represents one ten while the 6 represents six ones.

digital time

Time displayed as on a digital clock, either as 12-hour or 24-hour time.

dividend

The number that is divided in a division sum, e.g. in $12 \div 6 = 2$, 12 is the dividend. See also *divisor, quotient*.

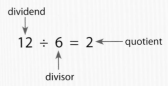

division (on a scale)

The intervals on a scale, on a ruler or a graph axis.

division bracket

The half box around the dividend in a division. See also *dividend*.

divisor

The number that is used to divide in a division sum, e.g. in $12 \div 6 = 2$, 6 is the divisor. See also *dividend, quotient*.

E

edge

The line made where 2 faces of a 3-D shape meet. See also *face, vertex*.

eighths

The fraction of a whole obtained when it is cut into 8 equal pieces.

equivalent

When 2 amounts are the same, but they could look different. 5 + 15 is equivalent to 20, $\frac{1}{2}$ is equivalent to $\frac{2}{4}$.

F

face

A flat surface on a 3-D shape. See also *edge* and *vertex*.

factor

Numbers that divide exactly into a number are its factors, e.g. the factors of 12 are 1, 2, 3, 4, 6, 12.

frequency table
A table showing how
often something occurs.

Travel	Tally	Frequency
Walk	ЦНІ ЦНІ ІІ	12
Car	ЦНІ ІІІІ	9
Bicycle	ІІ	2
Bus	ІІІ	3
Taxi	ІІ	2

G

gram
Symbol: g. a measure of mass or weight. There are 1000
grams in a kilogram. See also *kilogram*.

greater than
Also called more than. Symbol: >. Used when comparing
2 numbers or measures, e.g. 10 is greater than 7, or 10 > 7.
See also *less than*.

greatest value, least value
The highest or lowest value that can occur.

H

hemisphere
Half of a sphere.

hexagonal
Like a hexagon. A 2-D shape
with 6 straight sides.

horizontal
Going from side to side like the horizon. See also *vertical*.

hundreds boundary
When counting from tens to hundreds, the hundreds
boundary is crossed.

I

inverse
Addition is the inverse of subtraction, e.g. 16 + 24 = 40,
40 – 24 = 16. Multiplication is the inverse of division, e.g.
4 × 12 = 48, 48 ÷ 12 = 4.

irregular
Not regular. A shape with sides and angles that are not equal.

K

kilogram
Symbol: kg. A measure of mass or weight. There are
1000 grams in a kilogram. See also *gram*.

kilometre
A metric measure of distance. 1 km = 1000 m.

L

less than
Symbol: <. Used when comparing 2 numbers or measures,
e.g. 7 is less than 10, or 7 < 10. See also *more than*.

litre
Symbol: l . A measure of capacity. 1000 millilitres = 1 litre.

M

mass
A measure of the amount of matter in an object.
Measured in grams (g), kilograms (kg) or tonnes (t).

measuring cylinder
A graduated cylinder for measuring volume and capacity
accurately.

mental calculation
Doing a calculation in your head, perhaps using
informal jottings.

metre
Symbol: m. A measure of length or height,
100 centimetres = 1 metre.

millimetre
A small measure of length. 10 mm = 1 cm.

minuend
The starting number in a subtraction calculation, e.g.
10 (the minuend) – 3 (the subtrahend) = 7
(the difference). See also *subtrahend, difference*.

multiple
A multiple is the product of 2 numbers, e.g. the multiples of
8 are 8, 16, 24, 32, and so on.

multiplicand
A number to be multiplied, e.g. in 6 × 3 = 18, 6 is the
multiplicand. See also *multiplier*.

multiplier
The multiplying number, e.g. in 6 × 3 = 18, 3 is the multiplier.
See also *multiplicand*.

N

numerator
The number of parts of the whole required. The number
above the vinculum in a fraction. See also *denominator*.

O

obtuse angle

An angle between 90° and 180°.
See also *acute, reflex angle*.

octagon, octagonal

A 2-D shape with 8 straight sides.

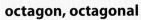

one hundred less/more

A number one hundred whole units more
or less than another number. 900 is a hundred
less than 1000 and 100 more than 800.

P

parallel

Lines that are the same distance apart and never meet.

pentagon, pentagonal

A 2-D shape with 5 straight sides.

perimeter

The total distance around the outside of shape.

perpendicular

Lines that are at right angles to each other. Horizontal lines
are always perpendicular to vertical lines.

polygon

The general name for 2-D shapes with straight sides. Includes
triangle (3 sides), quadrilateral (4 sides), pentagon (5 sides)
and so on.

polyhedron

The general name for 3-D shapes with straight sides. Plural
polyhedra. Includes tetrahedron, prisms, pyramids, and so on.

p.m.

From Latin post-meridian, meaning after midday. See also
12-hour time.

prism

A 3-D shape with 2 identical and
parallel ends, joined by rectangular
faces. The cross-section of a prism is
always the same as the ends.

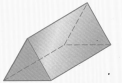

product

The result of multiplying 2 numbers. The product of 4 and 3
is 4 × 3 = 12.

Q

quadrilateral

A 2-D shape with 4 straight sides.

Rectangles, squares and kites are special sorts of quadrilaterals.

quotient

The answer to a division calculation, e.g. in 12 ÷ 6 = 2, 2 is the
quotient. See also *dividend, divisor*.

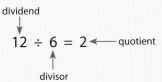

R

rectangle

A 2-D shape with 4 straight sides. A square is a regular
rectangle and oblong is sometimes known as an irregular
rectangle.

regular

A 2-D shape with all the sides equal length and equal angles.

remainder

The number left over after a division sum, e.g. in 13 ÷ 3 = 4
remainder 1.

right angle

A quarter of a full turn. 90°.

Roman numerals

Numbers used by the Romans. Digits have no place value,
e.g. II = 2 , VI = 6, LX = 60.

round up, round down

A method of approximation. 37 rounds up to the nearest 10
so gives an approximation of 40, but 34 rounds down to the
nearest 10 so gives an approximation of 30. Digits 4 or less
round down and digits 5 or more round up, so 750 to the
nearest 100 is 800.

rule

An instruction for carrying out a mathematical operation or continuing a pattern. It can be written using symbols or words. See also *sequence*.

S

second

Symbol: s. A measure of time.

sequence

A set of numbers made by following a given rule, e.g. the multiples of 3 are 3, 6, 9 and so on.

sevenths

The fraction of a whole obtained when it is cut into 7 equal pieces.

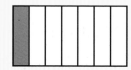

sixths

The fraction of a whole obtained when it is cut into 6 equal pieces.

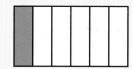

statement

A mathematical sentence, e.g. all even numbers are multiples of 2.

subtrahend

The number that is subtracted from the minuend. See also *difference, minuend.*

sum

The answer to an addition calculation. The sum of 4 and 5 is 9. See also *total*.

symmetry, symmetrical

A figure has line symmetry if it can be folded along a mirror line into 2 identical halves, which are mirror images of each other.

line of symmetry

T

tenths

The fraction of a whole obtained when it is cut into 10 equal pieces.

title

A sentence to describe or explain a chart, graph or diagram.

total

The answer to an addition calculation. The total of 4, 3 and 5 is 12. See also *sum*.

triangular prism

A 3-D shape with 2 identical and parallel triangular ends, joined by 3 rectangular faces.

U

units

The position in a number where the digit represents units, e.g. in 278 there is a digit 8 in the units place, so there are 8 units.

V

Venn diagram

A way of representing information.

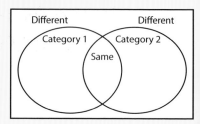

vertex, vertices

The point where 2 or more lines or edges intersect. See also *face, edge.*

vertical

A line that is perpendicular to a horizontal line. See also *perpendicular.*

vinculum

The line that separates the numerator and denominator in a fraction.

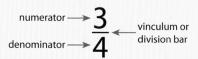

W

whole/part relationship

Parts of the whole. In the fraction $\frac{2}{3}$, the whole has been divided into 3 equal parts and we are thinking about 2 of those parts. When thinking of an addition calculation, e.g. 54 + 46 = 100, 54 and 46 are the parts and 100 is the whole. There are many whole-part relationships in mathematics.

written calculation

A mathematical operation done formally as a vertical written method.